Saint-John Perse

PRAISE AND PRESENCE

by

Pierre Emmanuel

With a Bibliography

Published for the Library of Congress by the
Gertrude Clarke Whittall Poetry and Literature Fund

LIBRARY OF CONGRESS • WASHINGTON • 1971

Library of Congress Cataloging in Publication Data

Emmanuel, Pierre.
    Saint-John Perse: praise and presence.
    Lecture delivered Dec. 2, 1968, under the auspices of the Gertrude Clarke Whittall Poetry and Literature Fund.
    "Saint-John Perse: a list of his writings in the collections of the Library of Congress . . . compiled by Ruth S. Freitag": p.
    1. Léger, Alexis Saint-Léger, 1889–
I. Freitag, Ruth S. II. U.S. Library of Congress. Gertrude Clarke Whittall Poetry and Literature Fund. III. Title.
PQ2623.E386.Z68   848'.9'1209   72-174226
ISBN 0–8444–0006–8

For sale by the Superintendent of Documents, U.S. Government Printing Office, Washington, D.C. 20402 - Price 45 cents
Stock Number 3000–0053

THE GERTRUDE CLARKE WHITTALL
POETRY AND LITERATURE FUND

The Gertrude Clarke Whittall Poetry and Literature Fund was established in the Library of Congress in December 1950, through the generosity of Mrs. Gertrude Clarke Whittall, in order to create a center in this country for the development and encouragement of poetry, drama, and literature. Mrs. Whittall's earlier benefactions include the presentation to the Library of a number of important literary manuscripts, a gift of five magnificent Stradivari instruments, the endowment of an annual series of concerts of chamber music, and the formation of a collection of music manuscripts that has no parallel in the Western Hemisphere.

The Poetry and Literature Fund makes it possible for the Library to offer poetry readings, lectures, and dramatic performances. This lecture, and the accompanying bibliography, are published by the Library to reach a wider audience and as a contribution to literary history and criticism.

Contents

Saint-John Perse

PRAISE AND PRESENCE

Penetrating the work of a great poet requires an effort of renunciation. One must escape from one's own personality and become another person, if that is possible. One must subject oneself not only to a new rhythm but also to the energy which produces it and singularizes it. The energy of a temperament? This is saying too little. In a strong work, the history of its creator is apparent, although it is sometimes obscure even to himself. What beats in the meter is the pulse of a destiny; and *destiny* presupposes a total conception of man, a unitarian relationship between the poet and the human form, whether he has recourse to it or whether he creates it. This human form lives in the language; it imposes its rhythm upon it and communicates it to the reader. Reading a great poet, not just superficially but the whole of his work, means inevitably coming to grips with this form and conforming to it so as to know it better, which may mean resisting it more strongly. As every creator is vitally bound to his own conception of man, the effort of understanding it and identifying oneself with it is a demanding one, particularly if the reader is a poet himself. He cannot, without risking his own form, travel too far out of himself toward the other person; at least the demands he has to make upon himself will force him to assess his own belief in relation to a belief which is partially or totally other.

Those who are shocked by the word "belief" in a context of aesthetic judgment do not know or do not want to know to what degree, far beyond what he may appear to be in the eyes of others or even in his own eyes, a poet commits himself in the word which carries him forward and out of himself. By committing himself, he commits man. The work of Saint-John Perse, dominated by the image of the sea, is one of man's voyages of discovery around man; it is one of man's attempts beyond himself, toward himself; it is also the vehicle, the carrier wave

1

of this adventure of the spirit. It will be seen from what I have to say about this work that I have followed it with active sympathy as far as I could, but my unknown lands are not those of the poet of *Anabase.* In the spiritual field, the unknown, for some, is that part of the real which still escapes extreme and constant attention from the mind; it is therefore something human, potentially; nothing but human. For others, the unknown is the Being in its plenitude which constantly besets the spirit with a mysterious *absence-presence* whose voice in the midst of all things is this poignant, divine incognito. These are two very different prospects, two breachings of man in apparently opposite directions: one is expansion toward the periphery of the known, the other is interrogation of the being at its center. These movements may alternate in the same poet; one of them may remain inconceivable for him, or, sometimes, it may be consciously rejected as meaningless. With Saint-John Perse, the rejection of movement toward the interior strikes me all the more since, at first, it seems to liberate considerable creative energy, indefatigably occupied with the sensuous externalization and the complex abundance of forms. Only later do I see it as a well of silence beneath their exuberant din.

This work, in its architecture, or rather its development as a whole, seems to be arranged almost exclusively within the circular space of the eye which takes the measure of everything: the sea, the wind, the distance traveled by men, their history, and their manner of being are unfolded horizontally. In *Chronique,* however, the notion of the verticality of spiritual space is introduced, almost surreptitiously, no longer as a simple part of the landscape but as the expression of a possible relationship. With what or with whom outside the universe of man? We shall try to define this later. Here, it is enough to note a new direction—the sky, perhaps the void—even if, immediately, the horizontal dimension—the sea, the islands—resumes its almost exclusive role in the vision. The all-embracing circular gaze balances and maintains the world under the sole domination of man. Every height, even that of the mountain peaks or the clouds, remains level with his forehead.

Lève la tête, homme du soir. La grande rose des ans tourne à ton front serein. Le grand arbre du ciel, comme un nopal, se vêt en Ouest de cochenilles rouges. Et dans l'embrasement d'un soir aux senteurs d'algue sèche, nous éduquons, pour de plus hautes transhumances, de grandes îles à mi-ciel nourries d'arbouses et de genièvre.

Horizontal and vertical at the same time, such is this soaring gaze.

The most faithful and encompassing image of the human spirit, worthy, according to Saint-John Perse, of crowning its poetical edifice, is, of course, the bird. A text inspired by Braque's *Birds* was to give the poet an opportunity to crown his work by soaring above the idea he had formed of the creative act, inseparable from the created thing. In this deliberately didactic poem, the poet seizes and defines not only Braque's spirit, in its progress, but also the progress of his own spirit. This definition, an aesthetic one, professes resolute antisymbolism. If "the bird, of all our consanguineous creatures, the most avid to live, of all our commensal the most avid to be," exists only by carrying itself to the extreme of its passion to live, by consuming itself, it does nothing more than obey its material law.

Rien là de symbolique: simple fait biologique. Et si légère pour nous est la matière oiseau, qu'elle semble, à contre-feu du jour, portée jusqu'à l'incandescence. Un homme en mer, flairant midi, lève la tête à cet esclandre: une mouette blanche ouverte sur le ciel, comme une main de femme contre la flamme d'une lampe, élève dans le jour la rose transparence d'une blancheur d'hostie...

Even as he rejects the symbol, Saint-John Perse impresses the image more strongly in its visible substance; and of this "visible," in a way widened and enriched of itself by a more subtle manner of *seeing,* he makes the Host, the sacrament of human presence in the world. Man is, preeminently, he who sees: only that which is seen by man is real. Braque's birds, entirely created by him "nearer the genus than the species, nearer the order than the genus," are visions. These visions are coexistent with external reality but extend it into a reality which is constantly being increasingly humanized—the creative dream.

Tout synthétiques qu'ils soient, ils sont de création première et ne remontent point le cours d'une abstraction. Ils n'ont point fréquenté le mythe ni la légende: et, répugnant de tout leur être à cette carence qu'est le symbole, ils ne relèvent d'aucune Bible ni Rituel.

The symbol, for Saint-John Perse, is not therefore a mediatory sign, but its use is a confession of incapacity. He who is not content with a thing in itself and reduces it to being nothing more than the shadow of a divine unreality—and there can be no doubt that this is what the poet means by the inefficiency of the symbol, the vampire which anemiates the real—dispossesses reality of its inherent mystery, which is nothing more than its indefinitely describable and nameable wealth. There is no ultimate mystery, no supernatural governing and exceeding life. Braque's birds derive from life and life alone.

Oiseaux sont-ils, de faune vraie. Leur vérité est l'inconnue de tout être créé. Leur loyauté, sous maints profils, fut d'incarner une constance de l'oiseau.

Let us, without questioning the poet, ignore the expression "tout être créé" (every created being). When we are not dealing with a human work, the idea of creation refers to some eternal (or continual) creative power. It is precisely this continuity in time and space, this living substratum of any evolution that is the most frequently evoked by Saint-John Perse, without referring to it otherwise than by the forces he brings into play—the wind, the tide, and the thought of man. All that can be reached, seen, and felt, if not seized, through its perpetual metamorphosis, is a process, or to use a nobler phrase, a state of flux, of "becoming." Human creation is part of this universal movement; it is an analogical component of it; its law is that of the Whole. Of his poems, as of Braque's birds, Saint-John Perse could say:

Dans la maturité d'un texte immense en voie toujours de formation, ils ont mûri comme des fruits, ou mieux comme des mots: à même la sève et la substance originelle. Et bien sont-ils comme des mots sous leur charge magique: noyaux de force et d'action, foyers d'éclairs et d'émissions, portant au loin l'initiative et la prémonition.

Thus, the word has the same origin, or even further, the same substance as the other material sources of energy. Between the world which exists before language and that which the word of the poet creates, there is indeed, as in Claudel's "L'Esprit et l'eau," something which persists, identical, and which supports something new. The difference between creation for Claudel and cosmic flux for Saint-John Perse does not prevent the idea from being shared by them both, through a gradual penetration or increase of the spirit throughout the world. But with Claudel, this penetration presupposes a movement of God toward man, initiating the movement of man toward God, whereas for Saint-John Perse, even though the whole of space is "crossed by a single thought," the finality of this thought is uncertain. Claudel considers creation as a hierarchical continuity, a universe which is entirely shaped in the mind of God and which opens itself to man so that he may capture it—along with God—in the "immense toils" of knowledge. On the contrary, the universal flux, so strongly marked in *Oiseaux,* is a dream whose internal finality escapes us in spite of the external logic we discover in it and sometimes we impose upon it.

Sur l'orbe du plus grand Songe qui nous a tous vus naître, ils passent . . . Avec toutes choses errantes par le monde et qui sont choses au fil de l'heure, ils vont où vont tous les oiseaux du monde, à leur destin d'êtres créés... où va le mouvement même des choses, sur sa houle, où va le cours même du ciel, sur sa roue—à cette immensité de vivre et de créer dont s'est émue la plus grande nuit de mai, ils vont, et doublant plus de caps que n'en lèvent nos songes, ils passent, nous laissant à l'Océan des choses libres et non libres...

One image however might make us think that the artist, the creator of forms in which the beginningless and endless dream shapes and amplifies itself, expanded and concentrated at the same time, is, as it were, enclosed because of his vocation in a focal point, a source, the face of which, as shown by the poet, could suitably represent one of the aspects of the thought of God.

Au point d'hypnose d'un œil immense habité par le peintre, comme l'œil même du cyclone en course—toutes choses rapportées à leurs causes lointaines et tous feux se croisant—c'est l'unité enfin renouée et le divers réconcilié.

This mystic, cyclopean eye which dreams of everything in everything appears from time to time and from afar in the work of Saint-John Perse. Is it the sun? It is probable. But it could also be the source of resolution (in the musical sense) at which paradoxes cease to be contradictory, that point of the spirit about which André Breton once wrote: "everything leads us to believe that it exists." It is true that for Saint-John Perse this point is "a point of hypnosis," the rent of the blue like an eye in the center of the cyclone. Matter never ceases to be animated by a movement which gives it form, by a succession of forms which multiply and destroy each other: at least thought is capable at every moment of seizing the appearance (facies). When the poet uses this word, he takes care to define its technical meaning: "used in geology to encompass historically, and as an evolutive whole, all the constituent elements of an identical matter during its formation." The eye of the painter therefore fixes and hypnotizes real movement. Each line, each suspended image, contains the whole of the movement in its curve, from its beginning to its end. The image of the eye which one might have been tempted to enlarge into a symbol of divine omnipresence, in which, because of his poetical predestination, the painter would have participated, is reduced to more modest proportions. What it expresses in fact is not a mysterious ubiquity but a discipline of attention. Saint-John Perse finds the true measure of the spirit in the order of facts; and, of these, dream (Songe) is nothing more than the complete development of that order in an awareness which is gifted with imaginative sensitivity and which because of it perceives more, associates better, and extrapolates further in duration. If the "supernatural," a word which is used extremely rarely by the author of *Anabase*, appears once in *Oiseaux*, it would be hasty to believe that it refers to anything other than "knowledge pursued like a piece of research and nature at last joined by the spirit after giving it everything." This recognition, as perceived, remains unknown in its principle and in its end, but, neither more nor less than the truth of any created being, it is both perceivable and unfathomable. Everything is contained "in its fact and in its fatality." The latter could also be called constancy or loyalty, for example, which express the persistence of this thing in its being and its fidelity, in the metamorphosis, to itself and to the Whole. When Saint-John Perse writes of Braque, "A long submission to the fact will have saved him from the arbitrary, without preserving him from the nimbus of the supernatural," he is not making a distinction between this submission and this mysterious fidelity; he is linking them together. In other words, the creative will of the painter, his power of attention and the plasticity of this attention when it comes into contact with things, constitute the *supernatural of nature,* the passage of nature beyond its own limit. This is why the bird created by the painter "follows him towards a new world without in any way severing its links with its original environment." When Saint-John Perse speaks of "renouement," of a unity at last "renewed," he does not imply an original rupture, nor a primordial fracture of the One, but simply that the diverse is connected in the thought of man and particularly so in that observer, the artist. It is the artist who, "free and not free," receives his talent and draws from it a definition of his task: to name the world as exhaustively as possible for the sole pleasure of living in it better, of pushing the world and the spirit which is inseparable from it to the extreme of their common possibility. The whole of Saint-John Perse's work is the proclamation and illustration of a self-sufficient aesthetic humanism, of an optimistic agnosticism which entrusts itself or at least abandons itself to the cosmic process in which the mind shares and whose rules it sometimes understands. The joy of speaking, the joy of creating, which correspond to the will to act, are alone sufficient to justify praise which is addressed only to things or which is only an overabundant manifestation of the being in the talons of energy. This praise does not transcend the world; it is inscribed in human facts. At a certain level of the spirit, it is the exact natural transcription of these facts. Through it, the world attains its own inherent plenitude, revealed by the spirit.

———————————◆◆◆———————————

The aesthetic set out in *Oiseaux*—Saint-John Perse's latest work—is consistent with the whole of his work since his adolescence. We may summarize its main postulates: the object of poetry is the *visible,* i.e., everything which may be perceived and explored by the senses; the poetic image is a vigilant refusal of the symbol, the fruit of an exhaustive attention to things, to their presence, their emanation, the relationships that the imagination seizes between them or establishes in its capacity as a function of the real. This extreme effort of the imagination to capture potential reality constitutes the state of praise whose exercise (which carries potentiality into reality, the real into the language and this language into the real) is creation, poetry. Poetry draws from the real a magic which is inseparable from it, since it is its *life* in all its forms, the constantly changing balance between the vital environment and the "living thing . . . taken from the living heart of the native tissue." Consequently, the poet, compared with other living beings, has no particular status of "interiority"; he too is placed completely inside the relationships and metamorphoses which he observes around him and in him. In fact, his capacity for attention gives him an impersonal ubiquity, a kind of "fourth dimension" of the mind to which the poem *Oiseaux* alludes. Art is "a moving and long meditation" which attempts to embrace life itself, in its supple organic complexity and its wonderful homology. At this degree of identification, of knowledge, the real allows itself to be perceived no longer as an order of definite facts but as an immense cosmic dream in which the poet participates by praising, i.e., by dreaming this dream aloud.

"O! j'ai lieu de louer!" This apostrophe from "Pour fêter une enfance" could well be an epigraph for the whole of the poet's work and life. Not only is praise a vocation and duty for him, it also flows from the place which situates him, the landscape and memory of childhood, the personal destiny and history of men, the cosmic ambition of the spirit. This place, which is both space and time, is completely filled with human presence. By diversifying it, this presence extols it and, conversely, this diversity praises the presence which constantly rouses it; praise is the place of man. Between *Eloges* and *Chronique,* the development of praise is continuous and its space-time never ceases to grow. It is as if the poet were undergoing—and pursuing—an ever deeper but less and less personal experience of duration. It begins with the static perfection of the memory of childhood and ends, in the evening of age, with "the appointment made . . . with that hour of grand meaning," the threshold beyond which "a loftier adventure is already being sung." An adventure, a conquest of lands for the mind, a vigil at the prow of the being, a lucidly creative flux (devenir) counterbalancing the great cosmic keel, such is human, personal, and planetary life for the poet both innumerable and alone. The manifestations of elemental energy correspond to the movements and seasons of the species and the spirit. The wind and the water—forces of transformation—play their role of motor and link in the universal genesis of forms. But being both here and elsewhere at the same time, they goad man into an indefinite widening of his powers; and the same is true for open space, desert or plain, submerged by the great floods of history through which, periodically, the geography of peoples is reshaped.

Dreamed in *Anabase,* planetary history is lived in those poems written in time of war: *Exil, Pluies, Neiges.* Fundamentally, they keep the same impersonality. War is a cataclysm only in the manner of telluric events: a manifestation of specific energy, exhilarating even in the destruction which, sundering hardened forms, liberates new origins. Of all the works of Saint-John Perse, none celebrates catastrophe with more optimistic rapture than *Vents.* Man, in his eternal quest which brings together in the mind the active or latent powers of the world, must reconcile himself with everything, even the worst, in order to remain united with the Whole. The agnosticism of Saint-John Perse forbids him to name the ultimate mystery; it does not prevent him from believing in a conjoined meaning, even if unrevealed, which is shared by man and the universe. After *Vents,* a liturgy of the destructive and fertile violence which governs the historical change of age, *Amers* is a poem about man carried beyond himself and confronting, as at a frontier, the eternal mirror of his destiny, the Sea, the intimate shadow and ultimate limit of being.

Commenting upon the thematic content of *Amers,* the poet wrote: "J'ai voulu exalter, dans toute son ardeur et sa fierté, le drame de cette condition humaine, ou plutôt de cette *marche* humaine, que l'on se plaît aujourd'hui à ravaler et diminuer jusqu'à vouloir la priver de toute signification, de tout rattachement suprême aux grandes forces qui nous créent, qui nous empruntent ou qui nous lient." These are the forces of permanent, demanding unsatisfaction from which the mind forms and which, at the same time, it provokes: before the sea, there is a duel between man and the element, between man and the self which is his own matter, in order to cross a decisive ford, in order to transgress a limit which constantly refers the spirit back to the human. Here, we must mention a divine instance to which, in the last resort, man appeals: an absolute in which he recognizes but fails to find himself. *Chronique* suggests that the ford to this absolute is death, unnamed, mediatory perhaps toward the secret of the enigma: here death is identified with the sea. Or, could it be that the ford is unnecessary, that the true way to the absolute is creative power, the spirit of the poet whose analogue is

8

the bird? With *Oiseaux,* victory over death and over time, whose impatience it is, seems to be acquired in the serenity of an overall curve—"orbe du plus grand Songe"—to which is linked, through the effort and flight of a beautiful work, that part of eternity the artist has received the gift to dream.

Such, in the firmament of sixty years, is the curve and life of the work. We must now study the word which carries it, the rhetoric of its speech. This word constitutes an independent space and an independent duration, through the enlargement and verbal amplification of a personal sensibility whose powers are goaded by a will to express itself. A sur-real is thus invented out of the real itself, which it embraces without being reduced by it. Let us open *Eloges.* In it, art is already performing its strict transmutation. The present, by establishing itself in the heart of a childhood past, intensifies it with a poetic, i.e., a subtly modulated nostalgia which reveals the magic processes of the word with a view to eternizing what is happening and extricating from temporal agitation the rhythm of eternity.

Alors, les hommes avaient
une bouche plus grave, les femmes avaient des bras plus lents;
alors, de se nourrir comme nous de racines, de grandes bêtes taciturnes
s'ennoblissaient;
et plus longues sur plus d'ombre se levaient les paupières...
(J'ai fait ce songe, il nous a consumés sans reliques.)

The solemnity of words, the slowness of gesture, the natural relationships between man and other living beings, between the spirit and space; the inborn perception of a common measure, of a form containing the various movements, a perfect place in which nothing is out of place, in which everything is exalted by being bound together: such is, from the first work, the atmosphere of the poetic "dream" in which the real, without being distorted, is elevated to the rank of the marvelous. Memory leaves no affective vestige, no regret, no "relic." It is consumed with him who recreates it. This recreation is a spiritual combustion. In this way, memory is reborn a phoenix. Set in the amber of perfection, the past becomes an image-object, an everlasting thing in the eternal order of things. It may be magnified in the present, just as the future is by means of prophetic projection, a visionary gift deepened by the vast simplification of the epic. Typified by the fullness and lightness of the vocables, by a sustained prosody in which the Alexandrine and other classical meters play a supporting role within a period or even a line, and by repetitive elements, enumerations, litanies, and long, exhaustive, and identically measured phrases, the style of Saint-John

Perse is so well developed in *Eloges* that the poet was to expand its processes later without appreciably increasing their number or improving upon its initial perfection. One might be tempted, as is often the case when one is faced with the first work of a great poet, to prefer to later overabundance the density and cohesion of this blossoming rhetoric which contains a great verbal space without ever being overwhelmed by it.

The first poem of *Eloges*, "Ecrit sur la porte," begins with the pronoun "Je."

> *J'ai une peau couleur de tabac rouge ou de mulet,*
> *j'ai un chapeau en moelle de sureau couvert de toile blanche.*

The person speaking is a mulatto. He speaks, in the present, of what surrounds him, of what he possesses or loves. He accompanies his gestures with words. He is an observer who reseizes and redoubles through the word his own reality and that of the world. Projecting this verbal shadow, every attitude, every movement unfolds a total act, a presence which conceives itself. A being who strives to be conscious of the manner in which he moves constantly seeks, through it, to give form to himself and therefore to his own universe. Almost invariably, when Saint-John Perse uses the pronoun "Je," he does so in this impersonal manner, identifying himself with such and such a present being, such and such a singular mode of presence. The poet possesses an unusual faculty of contemplative mimesis which enables him not to probe the souls of others—an unattractive proposition for this artist of the pure visible—but to take reality for the theater of a lucid dream which sharpens the real. To ennoble—a word which might define the poetic act according to Saint-John Perse—is in fact nothing other than to lift the real from its matrix, to reveal beauty as a law of the universe and a free aspiration of the spirit. To ennoble is to raise from the anonymous, to give a name and a form. The power of naming is indistinguishable from the attention given to that which is named by the vocable. The poet identifies himself with the object as much as he identifies it.

> *Appelant toute chose, je récitai qu'elle était grande, appelant toute bête, qu'elle était belle et bonne.*

Of all men, the poet is the narrator. He knows from memory and he speaks aloud according to a certain rhythm. What does he know? The beauty contained in the world, like the world's infancy.

> *—Sinon l'enfance, qu'y avait-il alors qu'il n'y a plus?*
> *Plaines! Pentes! Il y*

10

avait plus d'ordre! Et tout n'était que règnes et confins de lueurs.
Et l'ombre et la lumière alors étaient plus près d'être une même chose...

This is why in "Pour fêter une enfance" the "Je" of the child who will become the poet is both so personal and so universal. It is personal in a fresh way it never will be again; it is universal because childhood is an age at which awakening awareness is confused with the newborn world. An age without limits, without frontiers, at which the known and the unknown interpenetrate each other on the confines of the dream and the real. Paradoxically, man aspires to a similar state, at the extreme of his most lucid thought. No nostalgia of a paradoxical past affects the poetry of Saint-John Perse: from the early to the greatest age, the universe remains the same place of marvels, but a place in which the harmonious contentment of childhood blossoms into unsatisfaction which from a primordial intuition, the memory of the eternal, never ceases to produce newness both in man and the world. It might be thought that this maturing of creative unsatisfaction was hastened in Saint-John Perse by his departure from his native island, a break from an integrated universe. In *Eloges,* there is a certain dualism between the narrator and the child he still is, whom he refers to in the third person, as if he were someone he were observing. This dualism reaches its height in "Images à Crusoé," in which the poet, a prisoner of the capitals of Europe, imitates the old age of Crusoe projecting his island onto the wall opposite, through the casement. The identification with Crusoe cures the young man of his lost childhood by introducing him to the space of poetry, the place of eternal youth. Hence the importance of the poem "Le Livre," the last of the "Images à Crusoé," with which *Eloges* ends.

A choice is made, or a mutation takes place: the present, and no longer the past, is transfigured by the magic learned from childhood, this art of using words in such a way that the real, in embryonic form, springs from them. Just like Crusoe, Alexis Leger could not resign himself to losing the eternity of memory: just like Crusoe, he feels, moving in his heart, "the obscure birth of language" in which everything is concentrated and becomes one. The sea breeze, which is to take him toward that Promised Land both behind him and in front of him, is heard by Crusoe between the leaves of his Bible, the indivisibly divine and human Word in which all things are linked, from the first morning of the genesis to the cruel epic of Israel, from the "shouts" of God to the curses of the prophets. In the same way, Saint-John Perse guessed that the "privileged condition" of childhood could be restored in later age by the one who transfers to the poetic word the faith he has in the real. Man was created to sing his own epic, which exists only when it is sung. Deliberately, at the age of 18, in order to eternize the genius of childhood, Saint-John Perse chose continued dazzlement, the indefatigable migration toward the Void, at the very limit of the human. The whole of his work confirms this choice: it illustrates the will of the poet, even in the limits it imposes upon him and the grandeur it has to sustain.

———————————•◆•———————————

Henceforth, his work will be governed by the profound rhythms of history, the events of which, however much they may disrupt our lives, are nothing but weaker or stronger beats. "Réintégré comme Maître du Chœur, éclairant, soutenant et guidant l'action de ce très vaste déroulement humain," the Poet is, with the Prince, one of the protagonists of this fundamental risk, the cosmic genesis of man. It is only gradually that he becomes the pontiff of a liturgical and magic action, of an intercession with the universal Being, the principle of force and knowledge whose most exhilarating aspect is the sea. In "Amitié du Prince," which heralds *Anabase*, the Poet is still nothing more than the confidant of the King, who is alone in possessing charismatic qualities. The King is subtle, surrounded by signs; his nature has something of the feminine, a relationship with the elemental forces: he is gifted with divinatory dreams. Although he is placed among men, he is alone, the assessor of the supreme Power. He is dependent on them alone and they are all dependent on him. His function is to watch over the confines of man, at which the mind is constantly in conflict with itself, "fomenting a great quarrel at the highest point of the soul." The Poet still does nothing more than receive the innumerable praises of the people, but he is the "friend of the taciturn Prince" who calls him to him and who is honored by his counsel. A spiritual equality reigns between them: their common preoccupation concerns the things of the spirit, "Choses probantes et peu sûres." The King, in "Amitié du Prince," is motionless in the heart of his kingdom; it is he who is the observer. The Poet is the traveler who likes long journeys without a cause, "les longs déplacements sans cause." But the King is familiar with the same "torment of the spirit"; better still, he knows its source. And if he orders the Poet to hurry toward him, it is because he himself has things to do elsewhere. Consequently, their meeting, in the immense peace of the evening, the image of a well-governed country, seems to suspend the solemnity of a presage at the zenith of the heavens.

This meeting is also a prelude to the identification of the Poet and the Prince, or their symbiosis in the person of the "Etranger." It is the "Etranger" who spreads the clamor of the world: he liberates a wish to be in action and the "desires of the spirit" discussed by the Poet and the King. Later in the work, he is matched by another enigmatic figure, the "Etrangère." In *Amers* this name will be that of the Sea, "this other face of our dreams":

la chose sainte à son étiage, la Mer, étrange, là, et qui veillait sa veille d'Etrangère—inconciliable, et singulière, et à jamais inappariée—la Mer errante prise au piège de son aberration.

In this description of the Etrangère, we are able to recognize the same features with which "Amitié du Prince" defined the King. This is the proof of a mysterious complicity, a "co-naturality" between the adventurer of the spirit, the creator of new values "Sans-coutume-parmi-nous, ô Dissident" and "the sea in the morning like a presumption of the mind" inscribed both in the heart of the world and in our own heart. The very materiality of this spiritual omnipresence underlines how much, in Saint-John Perse, the conquest and the subversion of the spirit are inseparable from the great forces at work in the universe—these are not reciprocal figures but aspects of a same reality in action. The "Etranger" is precisely he who is aware of it, a stranger among us because he is closer, "attentive to his afflatus"; i.e., to the most tenuous meaning of the Being; that, however, which unites itself the most directly with the total discourse of energy.

Perhaps the summit of Saint-John Perse's work remains *Anabase.* When I read it at the age of twenty, it exhilarated me like the barbaric spectacle of the Assyrian rooms at the Louvre Museum, the heritage of a grandiose if terrifying age of man. It is true that, at the time, we were living through a period which heralded, which indeed was already, the sinister dawn of an infinitely cruel mutation in the history of Europe and the whole world. The pure fresco of the conquests of Alexander (or any other great adventurer of history) that *Anabase* unfolded before my eyes seemed to me to be the spiritual reflection in retrospect, the sublimation into praise, of an implacable tragedy. My ambivalence with regard to history found in it sufficient matter to feed this taste for the epic which retains from the human adventure nothing more than a design of genius, the paraph of a single will across the whole earth. In *Anabase,* this singular will foments and articulates innumerable others. The beautiful relationship between genius and the receptive anxiety of men whose wait will receive its meaning from this relationship is expressed by the sequence: "Hommes, gens de poussière et de toutes façons," the first of these incantatory enumerations, so numerous in Saint-John Perse, dynamic

inventories made during the human march and showing its direction—
here, beyond the various aims of the quest, a frontier at which eternity
might begin.

One essential thing is to be noted: these anxious beings, at the fore-
front of the great historical phrase (even if they are seekers, "finders
of reasons to go elsewhere"), do not seek the truth: only action is
important; its uncertainty is exhilarating; doubt about the quest is a
part of the quest. No one has the right to take delight in nostalgia
for intimate immobility, to elude the vital impulse.

*Mon âme est pleine de mensonge, comme la mer agile et forte sous
la vocation de l'éloquence! L'odeur puissante m'environne. Et le
doute s'élève sur la réalité des choses. Mais si un homme tient pour
agréable sa tristesse, qu'on le produise dans le jour! et mon avis est
qu'on le tue, sinon*
    il y aura une sédition.

Anabase multiplies ceremonial images, the liturgy of taking part in a
unique act of conquest and foundation. To found a town, to define a
people, is to fix a limit: it is at the same time to leave it behind one, to
appeal once again to the unlimited. The alternation of "Je" and "Nous"
to express the insatiable appetite for an "elsewhere" underlines the relationship between the Etranger and those in whom he awakens the desire
to follow him; he is simultaneously of the same nature as they and of a
radically different substance, because of this strangeness which has trans-
formed him, transmuted him.

—Et l'Etranger tout habillé
    *de ses pensées nouvelles, se fait encore des partisans dans les voies du
silence: son œil est plein d'une salive,*
    *il n'y a plus en lui substance d'homme. Et la terre en ses graines ailées,
comme un poète en ses propos, voyage...*

Nothing is more beautiful than the imaginary landscapes of *Anabase,*
conceived in such a way and dreamed to such a degree of perfection that
the effort needed to leave them and take to the road again seems to be a
direct intimation of the absolute. The landscapes are dreamed and yet
they are real, the archetypes of our locatable areas: the concrete image
stretches from the landscape, grows and changes without ceasing to be
spatial, so as to include not only the space of men but also their duration.
A fine example of a phrase without caesura which stops neither for
inspiration nor for the mind is: "La terre vaste sur son aire roule à pleins
bords sa braise pâle sous les   cendres"—a phrase whose very length
expresses both distance and the irresistible succession of time and, finally,

human wandering which can go beyond the temporal order only by using time to escape from it.

Terre arable du songe! Qui parle de bâtir?—J'ai vu la terre distribuée en de vastes espaces et ma pensée n'est point distraite du navigateur.

———————◆•◆———————

When one reads the attack of the great hymns of Saint-John Perse, one has the feeling that the poet, like the bards of long ago or like many Celtic poets today, makes use of his afflatus to give birth to the voice; he begins by speaking until he is gradually overcome by the word. "A great poem born of nothing, a great poem made of nothing"—such is *Exil;* such too are the poems which follow. A preliminary incantation and an investment by a rhythm rather than by a thought precede the birth of the dominant idea, as if it were forced out into the open by this provocation. Thus in *Pluies:*

Chante, poème, à la criée des eaux l'imminence du thème,
Chante, poème, à la foulée des eaux l'évasion du thème.

In *Vents,* the Winds themselves rise up, elevating afflatus to a point at which its own force can sustain it. A comparison between the beginning of *Vents* and that of "l'Esprit et l'eau" is striking for anyone who wishes to feel the differences between the dynamics of the two poets but also between the spirituality of Saint-John Perse and that of Claudel. And yet they have one thing in common; they both choose the great natural energies as a vehicle of the spirit. In his imagery of the elemental, Saint-John Perse likes above all that which provokes action, transforms, throws beyond or suggests irresistible and endless movement. A comparative study of the theme of the sea in the two poets might show two different metaphysics at work, both different and, eventually, contradictory: the paths towards the transcendent in Claudel are not the roads of spiritual flight so dear to Saint-John Perse. Nor does history have the same meaning for each of them. With Claudel, in fact, it is, in a mysterious tension, both the history of this world and the communion of the saints. The metahistory of Saint-John Perse is only the participation of the mind in the vital impulse and the awareness it has of the dialectic relationship between destruction and creation at the great moments of mutation or cataclysm. The most obvious example of this conception of history may be read in the admirable invocation to the *Pluies*, "laveuses des morts dans les eaux-mères du matin." Every temporal catastrophe is a pitiless denudation which leaves men with nothing of their good conscience, their prestige, their historical continuity, their knowledge, or even their value. Right from the beginning, this enumerative, accumulative process, suggesting the implacably regular fall of the rains which destroy everything except reason, places this long sequence in a register of fierce jubilation in which humor is present everywhere. It looks as if the basic optimism of the poet were confirmed by the devastating enterprise in which he takes part by giving it verbal rhythm. This attitude, it must be said, is exactly the opposite of a certain modern nihilism for which Saint-John Perse felt a horror he never attempted to hide. If the logic of history is never questioned it is, I think, because reason itself is beyond contestation; the absurd, even if it is of man, is perceived as a challenge to what is progressive in this reason, a challenge which drives reason to rejoin its own eternal past. Thus, reintegration, one of the key words in the thinking if not the poetry of the poet, passes through the catastrophe in which man achieves his catharsis. Furthermore, this catastrophe, an uncontrollable human phenomenon, must be assumed and even wished by the creative spirit. To take part in catastrophe, or simply, through the prophetic eye, to see it come from afar and describe its movement in advance is perhaps the most profound and—who knows?—the most efficient way of being a creator.

Tout à reprendre. Tout à redire. Et la faux du regard sur tout l'avoir menée!

However, the words "reprendre" and "redire" are chosen to mark the permanence of a reality which is quite indestructible even though it may always need to be seized and expressed again. And, in fact, this is a major part of the poet's activity: to enumerate, to collect, to reformulate, indefatigably, through an indefinite renewal of the same unrecognizable and always identical image, the same simple substance of eternal, definitive man.

This is why, as the work develops, hardly changing any of its essentials, the most pregnant image is the sea which constantly exceeds itself without ever leaving its limits: an image of man, who is always true to himself and who carries within him his own infinity. *Amers* is a major hymn in praise of the sea, and also of man, its model and mirror. It is a hymn of total reconciliation and almost appeasement, if one may use this word to describe a poetry which leaves so little room for silence. The poem is conceived "comme l'arène solitaire et le centre rituel," "l'aire théâtrale" or "la table d'autel du drame antique," around which humanity and its cities are built and around which the slow procession of the choruses takes place. "La grande chose fériée," the Sea, is also the very celebration, the great feast of the spirit. Two of the finest pages written by the poet, one from *Exil* and the other from *Amers,* are in fact devoted to the correspondence of the spirit and the sea, the latter, as a whole, being the mirror and the vehicle of the former. As the work takes on fullness, the sea is associated more and more closely with the genesis of the creative Word, until it identifies itself with it in us. In *Exil,* three stanzas, each of which (if correctly uttered, by taking afflatus to the extreme of its capacity) physically overwhelms and exhausts the being, describe the sea first of all as an eternal historical exodus, then as the inexhaustible human inspiration over the world, and finally as the indefatigable "dépassement" of the personal spirit by oneself. In *Amers,* the "Je" is replaced by "Nous": it is the whole collectively which sings, each voice being carried by the others and containing them at the same time. And from this chorus around the sea the sea itself rises: it is the song, the energy shared by all men, the prophecy, the Supreme Word, which goes beyond them and yet is born of them.

So, as can be seen, the theme of the "Etrangère" matches that of the "Etranger": the sea is the soul of the Prince, or that of the Poet, that of the *griot* to whom are delegated, as to the King, the powers and the memory of the community. The strangeness of the Prince is sacral, given what his people unknowingly bears within itself: the same is true of the strangeness of the sea and the spirit, in the abyss that the human species is digging within itself. The sea rises "plus haut que notre face, à hauteur de notre âme" like the "Prince sous l'aigrette, comme la tige en fleurs à la cime de l'herbe." Around it, as around the Prince, are the characters of the epic, or the Greek drama, a procession—"Récitation en marche vers l'Auteur et vers la bouche peinte de son masque." Toward which author? Is it simply the tragic poet or, behind the mask of the sea itself, is it the God that Saint-John Perse never names directly except in *Chronique,* in which, ambiguously, the word might also refer to the sun? This is a fruitless question in fact since the poet never raises it; even if he guesses at it on our lips, he never answers except in *Chronique* and only then by an interrogation of the Void which in no way possesses the element of positive meaning sometimes contained in the idea of absence. And, until the end, throughout this work and over the sea itself, we shall hear, sure of itself, the ring of

> *le grand pas souverain de l'âme sans tanière,*
> *Comme aux dalles de bronze où rôderait un fauve.*

Can this—a pride, an impatience—be sufficient to justify life? The prisoner of its own circumsession, human infinity remains limited. So finally, and perhaps in spite of him when, at the very end of *Chronique,* the poet offers the heart of man, as on a paten, to the sky—since the vertical is the only really open dimension—this strange gesture, and its

17

place in the work, which gives it a definitive character, takes on a deeply moving significance, precisely because the reference to the wandering, great wild soul follows immediately.

L'offrande, ô nuit, où la porter? et la louange, la fier?... Nous élevons à bout de bras, sur le plat de nos mains, comme couvée d'ailes naissantes, ce cœur enténébré de l'homme où fut l'avide, et fut l'ardent, et tant d'amour irrévélé...

In this passage, everything calls for comment. Let us mention this "Nous" which in fact becomes a "Je" since this is the poet in the evening of his age, inscribing in his own experience the whole cycle of human existence. But, above all, we must note the use of the word "cœur," infrequent in Saint-John Perse. And yet it is the *heart* and not the *spirit* that the poet chooses to embrace—in a single vocable—the unity and totality of the human being: and further still, its *mystery,* connected by this ultimate oblation to some kind of supreme mystery or dominating reality. But the word "heart" also has a more immediate meaning as the seat of human love. Now if, in the thematic content of *Amers,* there is something really new compared with previous poems, it is the appearance in strength of this love in the poet's inspiration and the analogical reciprocity established between woman and the sea. Until this point—except in the images from childhood—woman had always remained almost exclusively "the warrior's rest"; her place was in man's desire and not in his thought. "Récitation à l'éloge d'une reine" had turned her into a barbaric idol comparable, in the human order, to the queen of a beehive. Only two short but poignant notations in *Exil* and *Neiges* revealed something else in the poet: a secret emotional life torn by exile.

Deux fronts de femmes sous la cendre, du même pouce visités; deux ailes de femmes aux persiennes, du même souffle suscitées...

But in *Amers,* the mother and the friend, just like the other more conventional figures which represent woman in the rest of the work, are entirely enveloped and overwhelmed by the great image of the *"Amante,"* who is to man what the sea is to the pilot of the ship. If, at times, one might find the verbal abundance of *Amers* somewhat excessive, there is one part of the poem which escapes this reproach: that which describes woman indivisible from the sea. This part contains a powerful eroticism connected with the major theme of the whole work: the omnipresent reign of the spirit. Even in the extreme expression of sensuality, the spirit never ceases its watch; in this way, it corresponds to woman's desire to be conquered each time. But if the woman, the "Amante," can say to the man she loves, "You are there, my love, and I have no other place than in you," she also knows that this man is from nowhere, or has no other place than his own solitude.

Comment aimer, d'amour de femme aimer, celui pour qui nul ne peut rien? Et d'amour que sait-il, qui ne sait qu'épier, au miracle du front, ce seul bonheur de femme qu'il suscite?...

This is an admirable expression of the difference—perhaps irreducible—between the two halves of human love, or rather between the instinct of totality which haunts woman and the obsession with unity which makes man, above woman, as he is above the world, the hawk that wants everything in its gaze and loves nothing except this gaze. This canticle of the "Amante" and the "Aimé," which alternates with the responses of man, is astonishingly a feminine word not placed by masculine imagination on the lips of woman but experienced by the poet in that feminine part of one's self revealed by the immense dialogue of *Amers*. This dialogue is entirely different from Claudel's unforgettable exchanges in which woman plays the role of the provoker forcing man to extenuate his own limits and consume himself with them in order to reach the absolute. In Saint-John Perse, woman remains fearful, contained, circumscribed by the design and destiny of man. She becomes the high seas only if he so wishes and if he gives her the necessary rhythm. Revealed to herself by man—the contrary of what happens in Claudel—she sees in the act of love (in which she allows herself to be penetrated to the depths of her being which she can in this way reach) the most accomplished form of the world's existence, the microcosm of the same forces which ceaselessly create and move the universe.

Et la femme est dans l'homme, et dans l'homme est la mer, et l'amour loin de mort sur toute mer navigue. . . .
Il n'est d'action plus grande, ni hautaine, qu'au vaisseau de l'amour.

In order to express such sentences, in which woman tries to define and, further still, protect her conception of the absolute in love, the poet uses a rigid Alexandrine with a strong median caesura, thus stressing, perhaps unconsciously, how fragile and arbitrary, in the very eyes of the woman who states it, is this possessive image of unity. In the caesura between man and woman, there is a beat other than that of the blood, the terrible pulse of the sea. It is only as a servant, having accepted in man the presence of another more powerful love, that the "Amante" may enfold within her the heart which fills her only if it overwhelms her. Only in this way may she say "of woman more than woman" to her lover.

Etroits sont les vaisseaux, étroite notre couche. Et par toi, cœur aimant,

toute l'étroitesse d'aimer, et par toi, cœur inquiet, tout l'au-delà d'aimer.
Entends siffler plus haut que mer la horde d'ailes migratrices. Et toi
force nouvelle, passion plus haute que d'aimer, quelle autre mer nous
ouvres-tu où les vaisseaux n'ont point d'usage?

What other sea? The formidable chorus which appears at the end of
the poem allows this question to arise without answering it, submerging
it immediately in the praise of which it is only one moment, even if, for
a fleeting second, it is the highest. It is true that the massive celebration
of the sea, wisdom, presence, power, splendor, divine fable, light made
substance, being surprised in its essence, measure and excess, incorporeal
and very real, place of all contradiction and principle of all unity, mag-
nifies in the heart of the world a reality of which the sea, which is
indivisible from it, is only the visible image and the constantly pro-
claimed tumult. "God the Undivided governs his provinces." God: is
this the name that, in the "smoke of the threshold," the poet gives to such
a reality? But it is only a name given by man, just like Baal, or Mam-
mon, or Dagon, also enumerated in *Amers*. Man dreams God in the
gods. Perhaps God dreams the man in man. The finale of *Amers*
evokes this great dream, the other face of which, immeasurable, remains
vertiginously unknown to us.

...C'est toi, Présence, et qui nous songes.
Nous te citons: "Sois là!" Mais toi, tu nous as fait cet autre signe qu'on
n'élude; nous as crié ces choses sans mesure.

"C'est toi, Présence": an impersonal reality and personal at the same
time by the very fact that it is called upon, celebrated. This "Tu" form,
which appears throughout the work, is always used to address a hypos-
tasis of the divine: here the divine behind its mask, and in its most
sublime personification, the Sea which hides and reveals, the symbolic
Being, in the fullest meaning, the only one to escape the poet's mistrust
of all symbols. We must admire how the poet, undecided between
adoration of the transcendent and pure dionysiac exaltation, stands both
before the supreme reality and the sea which is its veil and threshold:

Faut-il crier? faut-il prier?... Tu vas, tu vas, l'Immense et Vaine, et
fais la roue toi-même au seuil d'une autre Immensité...

Even if, in the last works of the poet, a question about the nature of
this *other* reality is present in embryonic and sometimes in almost complete form, more than ever, the real interrogation concerns man in

whom, in the final analysis, this other reality must be inscribed if it is worthy of being a question.

Nous passons, et, du nul engendrés, connaît-on bien l'espèce où nous nous avançons? Que savons-nous de l'homme, notre spectre, sous sa cape de laine et son grand feutre d'étranger?

By giving more and more fullness to a poem whose unique theme is the creative energy of man, connected with the world in which it is active and which it unifies, Saint-John Perse never exhausts, on the contrary he deepens and widens, the mysterious distance between us, as men, and the man in us, this Stranger. Stranger, Husband of the Sea, and "half-terrestrial" like his Spouse. After challenging the inadequacy of the symbol, the poet, when he has spent all his praise, once again experiences the inadequacy of any description: the more he has pushed back the limit, the more oppressive the circle is. The dialectic between the expansion of creative freedom and the growth of human anxiety is the driving force of this poetry. Anxious poetry, constantly moving, but not anguished: anxiety is a vector of praise. Perhaps, even, it is used indefinitely to avoid the solicitation of the symbol which, by awakening our inner anguish, might force us to appeal to the invisible for the visible and for the appearance of things to their hidden part. There is none of this in Saint-John Perse, who prefers the suspense of the unknown, the clean break of the long phrase which could only be prolonged elsewhere.

...Et sur le cercle immense de la terre, un même cri des hommes dans le vent, comme un chant de tuba... Et l'inquiétude encore de toutes parts... O monde entier des choses...

We remember having heard this "O monde entier des choses" somewhere else, but not suspended and incomplete in spite of the integrity it postulates; on the contrary unified, set in a hierarchy, linking heaven and earth, the sky and the abyss. It was in Claudel's "L'Esprit et l'eau."

Salut donc, ô monde nouveau à mes yeux, ô monde maintenant total! O credo entier des choses visibles et invisibles, je vous accepte avec un cœur catholique!

The principle of the "renouement" of man in Claudel is the spirit in its relationship with water, or rather the source of their symbolic relationship: a Word whose name is the Paraclete. Here, it is a question of relinking man to a reality from which he has disassociated himself: this "renouement" does not depend upon man alone, but on a love which transcends and reintegrates him. Saint-John Perse's ideas are quite different and one might wonder whether, in his mind, the "renouement" of man is anything other than a unification of his powers. Nothing in the poet of *Vents* suggests the idea of any original unity from which man might have fallen; rather must we see in his design of integration the asymptote of all human activities, with man extracting his unity from multiplicity, the indefinite diversity of men, this "anxiety of all parts" which the Prince and the Poet bring together into a single meaning, or rather the genesis of a meaning, that of man, this enigmatic Stranger.

Car c'est de l'homme qu'il s'agit, et de son renouement.
Quelqu'un au monde n'élèvera-t-il la voix? Témoignage pour
l'homme...
Que le Poète se fasse entendre, et qu'il dirige le jugement!

It would not be a misconstruction to interpret "diriger le jugement" as meaning to guide human reason in its project, or better still, to extract from reason the finality it creates for itself. This temptation to which the poet devotes himself is a purely humanist ambition that does not presuppose any external purpose, or at least any personal relationship with this purpose: the forward movement, the "dépassement," is justified in itself, although it may be guided by the poet, whose mysterious instinct is simply stated and, no doubt, participates in a universal Inexplicable, constantly praised and never identified. In the poetry of the author of *Anabase,* the individual human being is only very rarely faced with himself; he is nearly always contained within a mythical man whose only strongly marked characteristic is to be transcendent with regard to himself. In this abstract humanism lies the grandeur and the limit of Saint-John Perse. What is missing from his universe is the universal singular, the concrete being. The dimensions of suffering and evil, which alone establish the true depth of man and without which the march of history is reduced to a procession of bas-reliefs, are purposely silenced in this work in which, on the contrary, the sensuous wealth of the world is explored to the limits of our senses. Consequently, there is nothing in Saint-John Perse—not even a cry, although he often uses this word—which helps us to take the measure of the history we have lived. However beautiful the texts which are marked by war, their virtue is insufficient when it comes to evoking and exorcising the pure demoniac, that of totalitarianism and concentration camps. Men have an essential knowledge of this demoniac only through their own nature in which it is inscribed as a redoubtable virtuality, but Saint-John Perse, the navigator of the abysses (whether they are those of history, the sea, or the enigma of man himself), never forces us to refer to our inner abyss in order to question him. It is a pity that, in spite of his afflatus, this great poet, when it comes to the complexity of human nature, seems to lack daring, as it were. But in Saint-John Perse, these limitations are perhaps too openly admitted to be worthy of a long analysis. Even if thought, reduced to a summary metaphysics, often remains unsatisfied, the exuberant splendor of a constantly renewed imagination makes up for the insufficiencies of this being. In the absence of a word which expresses itself in degrees of silence and night, it is a lascivious, glittering language, lavish with its vital force, which stretches itself before our eyes and bathes in the sunlight: without always leading us to joy, its naked pleasure is intoxicating.

The fact that this splendor is also a lack and that this glitter is dazzling in no way prevents them from being an accomplished beauty in their order: nor does it prevent them, as Saint-John Perse constantly summons them up, from glorifying the Presence contained in everything but too large for any of its names. If Saint-John Perse has never tried to raise this anonymity in the center of Being, we must believe it is out of respect. Perhaps this same respect leads him deliberately to conceal man's predicament in the dazzle of this unique reality. If man takes an interest in man and extols him as he is, this is part of the universal praise in which this reality rejoices in itself: but Saint-John Perse cannot bring himself to believe that this reality is capable of taking a personal interest in every man, much less loving him. This limit imposed on love transforms the Presence into an Absolute hidden behind a cosmic illusion, and turns man into a contradictory being who tries (in vain?) to escape this illusion without feeling that any claims are being made by that Absolute upon him. Man can praise, if not love; he never feels that the Presence loves him. Finally, the poetry of Saint-John Perse is the expression of a sempiternal effort of praise, a challenge (since man only is if he is more) to the double silence of the Mayic universe and the immutable Absolute. Nothing can express better this effort and the formidable accumulated fatigue which he has to conquer than these two phrases in *Chronique,* the key perhaps to a great work and the great soul which animates it from beginning to end.

Nous sommes pâtres du futur, et ce n'est pas assez pour nous de toute l'immense nuit dévonienne pour étayer notre louange... Sommes-nous, ah, sommes-nous bien?—ou fûmes-nous jamais—dans tout cela?

Saint-John Perse

A LIST OF HIS WRITINGS IN THE

COLLECTIONS OF THE LIBRARY OF CONGRESS

INTRODUCTORY NOTE

Compiled by Ruth S. Freitag, head of the Bibliography and Reference Correspondence Section, General Reference and Bibliography Division, this list includes all writings published under the pseudonym Saint-John Perse or the author's own name, Alexis Leger, and other items attributed to him, that are represented by cards in the Library's Main Catalog. Citations are also given to poems, parts of poems, and essays published in journals before or simultaneously with their appearance as books or pamphlets and to poems and prose writings published only in journals or collections. Letters and memoranda in the Library's manuscript, rare book, and general collections are individually described and their contents summarized. Translations are listed for complete poems, and for parts of poems published in book form (e.g., item 78); translations of parts of poems in journals and anthologies are omitted. No attempt was made to collect references to musical settings, recordings, or pictorial material of any kind.

Arrangement of the entries is primarily chronological. Sections for the seven major poems or groups of poems are presented in the order of their first appearance and are followed by a section for collected editions. Entries in the three final sections are arranged chronologically by date of composition or, if this could not be determined, by date of publication. Translations are listed alphabetically by language after all entries for the French original.

It should be noted that the Archibald MacLeish papers and the Huntington Cairns papers, in the custody of the Manuscript Division, may be used only with the permission of Mr. MacLeish and Mr. Cairns respectively. Requests to use the papers in the Central Files should be addressed to the Chief, Central Services Division, Library of Congress, Washington, D. C. 20540.

Locations are shown by call numbers for cataloged works and by symbols for uncataloged works and for materials held by custodial units.

KEY TO SYMBOLS

CS	Central Services Division
DLC	Library of Congress (uncataloged)
Mss	Manuscript Division
N&CPR	Newspaper and Current Periodical Room
Rare Bk. Coll.	Rare Book Collection

ELOGES

1

Images à Crusoé.   Nouvelle revue française, t. 2, août 1909: 22–29.

AP20.N85, v. 2

Signed Saintléger Léger.

2

Eloges.   Nouvelle revue française, t. 3, avril 1910: 438–451.

AP20.N85, v. 3

Signed Saintléger Léger.
Contents.—Pour fêter une enfance.—Récitation à l'éloge d'une reine.—
Ecrit sur la porte.

3

Eloges.   Nouvelle revue française, t. 5, juin 1911: 810–831.

AP20.N85, v. 5

Signed Saintléger Léger.
In 18 untitled sections.

4

Chanson.   Commerce (Paris), no 3, hiver 1924:7.   AP20.C56, v. 1
Published in the 1925 edition of *Eloges* as the concluding poem, under
the title "Ecrit sur la porte," and in subsequent editions as "Chanson du
présomptif" in the section "La gloire des rois."

5

Eloges.   Paris, Gallimard, Nouvelle revue française [1925] [109] p. on
[109] leaves.   PQ2623.E386E3   1925a
Photocopy (positive).
Contents.—Ecrit sur la porte.—Pour fêter une enfance.—Eloges,
I-XVIII.—La gloire des rois: Récitation à l'éloge d'une reine.   Amitié du
prince.   Histoire du régent.—Images à Crusoé.—Ecrit sur la porte.

6

Berceuse.   Mesa, no. 1, autumn 1945: 24–26.   AP1.M4, no. 1
Published in the third edition of *Eloges* ([Paris] Gallimard [1948]
[120] p.   Not in LC) in the section "La gloire des rois."

7

Amitié du prince.   Avec un hommage par Renato Poggioli.   Milano,
All'insegna del pesce d'oro, 1959.   30 p.   facsim.   (Bateau books, n. 3)

PQ2623.E386A78   Rare Bk. Coll.

500 copies printed.   "Copia n. 7."
Bibliography: p. 25–30.

Translations

ENGLISH

8

Eloges, and other poems. The French text with English translation by
Louise Varèse and an introduction by Archibald MacLeish. [1st ed.]
New York, W. W. Norton [1944] 179 p.   PQ2623.E386E4
  French and English on opposite pages.
  Based on the 1925 French edition.
  With a note by the translator.
  A version of this translation of the final poem, "Ecrit sur la porte,"
first appeared in *Heart of Europe,* an anthology edited by Klaus Mann
and Hermann Kesten, p. 97–98 (New York, L. B. Fischer [1943]
PN6019.M24).

9

Eloges, and other poems. Translation by Louise Varèse.   [Rev.]
Bilingual ed. [New York] Pantheon Books [1956] 103 p. (Bol-
lingen series, 55)   PQ2623.E386E4 1956
  French and English on opposite pages.
  The French text is from the *Œuvre poétique* of 1953.
  With a note, newly written for this edition, by the translator.

SPANISH

10

Elogios y otros poemas. Versión castellana de Jorge Zalamea. [1. ed.]
México, B. Costa-Amic [1946] 102 p.   PQ2623.E386E44
  Based on the 1925 French edition.
  This translation of "Images à Crusoé" was published at the same time
in *El Hijo prodigo,* v. 11, feb. de 1946, p. 90–93 (AP63.H5, v. 11).

———— Another copy.   PQ2623.E386E44   Rare Bk. Coll.

ANABASE

11

Poème. Nouvelle revue française, t. 18, avril 1922: 414–415.

AP20.N85, v. 18

  Prefatory song of *Anabase,* signed * * *.

30

12

Anabase. Nouvelle revue française, t. 22, jan. 1924: 46–62.

AP20.N85, v. 22

Fragments.

13

Anabase. Paris, Nouvelle revue française [1924] [53] p.

PQ2623.E386A8   1924   Rare Bk. Coll.

627 copies printed. "Cinq cent cinquante exemplaires sur vergé baroque à barbes, dont cinquante exemplaires hors commerce numérotés de 1 à 50, et cinq cents exemplaires, numérotés de 51 à 550. Exemplaire N° 387."

14

Anabase. [New York] Brentano's [1945] [75] p.

PQ2623.E386A8   1945

"Note bibliographique sur les publications d'Anabase": p. [59]–[62].

Includes French texts of prefaces to Russian and German editions of *Anabase,* written respectively by Valery Larbaud and Hugo von Hofmannsthal, and, in English, T. S. Eliot's preface to the English edition.

——— Another copy.   PQ2623.E386A8   1945   Rare Bk. Coll.

15

Anabase. Ed. rev. et corr., augm. d'une bibliographie. [Paris] Gallimard [1948] [75] p.

4PQ Fr–851

"Note bibliographique sur les publications d'Anabase": p. [57]–[61].

In addition to the prefaces noted in the preceding item, includes, in Italian, that written by Giuseppe Ungaretti for an Italian edition.

Translations

DANISH

16

Anabasis. *In* Anabasis. Eksil. Overs. og med indledning af Thorkild Hansen. [København] Gyldendal, 1960. p. [27]–[72].

PQ2623.E386A813

17

Anabasis, a poem. With a translation into English by T. S. Eliot. London, Faber & Faber, 1930. 75 p.

PQ2623.E386A8   1930a   Rare Bk. Coll.

French and English on opposite pages.

With a preface by the translator.

"'This signed edition, printed on English hand-made paper, is limited to three hundred and fifty numbered copies. This copy is number 78. [Signed] T. S. Eliot."

Eliot's translation of Canto I first appeared in the *Monthly Criterion*, v. 7, Feb. 1928, p. 137–138 (AP4.C87, v. 7).

18

Anabasis, a poem. With a translation into English by T. S. Eliot. London, Faber & Faber, 1930. 75 p.   PQ2623.E386A8   1930

French and English on opposite pages.

With a preface by the translator.

19

Anabasis, a poem. With a translation into English by T. S. Eliot. [1st American ed.]   New York, Harcourt, Brace, 1938.   75 p.

PQ2623.E386A8   1938

French and English on opposite pages.

With a preface by the translator.

————— Another copy.   PQ2623.E386A8   1938   Rare Bk. Coll.

20

Anabasis, a poem. Translated by T. S. Eliot. [Rev. and corr. ed.]   New York, Harcourt, Brace [1949] 109 p.   PQ2623.E386A8   1949

French and English on opposite pages.

"The Works of St.-John Perse": p. 97–100.

With the 1930 preface and a note to the revised edition, both by T. S. Eliot, and English texts of the prefaces by Larbaud, Hofmannsthal, and Ungaretti.

————— Another copy.   PQ2623.E386A8   1949   Rare Bk. Coll.

21

Anabasis, a poem. Translated by T. S. Eliot. [3d ed.]   London, Faber and Faber [1959] 96 p.   PQ2623.E386A8   1959   Rare Bk. Coll.

French and English on opposite pages.

Bibliography: p. 73–79.

In addition to the prefaces and note included in the 1949 edition, contains a note by Eliot to this edition and an English translation of a review by Lucien Fabre which appeared under the title "Anabase" in *Nouvelles littéraires,* 23 août 1924, p. 4 (PQ2.N6, 1924).

GERMAN

22

Anabasis. Französisch und Deutsch. Mit einem Essay von T. S. Eliot. [Unter Benutzung der Erstfassung von Walter Benjamin, Bernard Groethuysen und Herbert Steiner übertragen von Friedhelm Kemp] München, R. Piper [1961] 74 p. (Piper Bücherei, 161)

PQ2623.E386A8 1961

French and German on opposite pages.

Bibliography: p. 74.

Parts of this translation—both songs and Cantos I and VII—were first published in *Jahresring* 55/56, p. 278–282 (Stuttgart, Deutsche Verlags-Anstalt [°1955] PT1141.J3, 55/56).

ITALIAN

23

Anabase, seguita dalle traduzioni di T. S. Eliot e Giuseppe Ungaretti. Illustrata da Berrocal. Verona, Le Rame, 1967. 131 p. 9 col. illus.

PQ2623.E386A8 1967 Rare Bk. Coll.

Issued in portfolio.

"Questa edizione . . . illustrata con nove incisioni in linoleum a colori di Berrocal, è stata impressa in occasione dell'ottantesimo compleanno dell'autore dalla Stamperia Valdonega di Giovanni Mardersteig, in carattere Bembo, sur carta a mano di Pescia, in centoventidue esemplari, novantanove dei quali numerati da 1 a 99 e ventitré, fuori commercio, segnati con le lettere A-Z. La legatura, in carta Roma di Fabriano, con due disegni dell'artista, stampati in rilievo sulla copertina, è stata eseguita da Giovanni de Stefanis. I linoleum, dopo la stampa, sono stati biffati. . . . Esemplare 78." Signed by the artist.

JAPANESE

24

Ensei. Mungen, quarterly magazine of poetry, dai 15-gō, shunki-gō 1964: 126–134. port. DLC

Translated by Rikutaro Fukuda.

This issue includes several other translations and a number of critical articles.

SERBO-CROATIAN

25

Anabasa. *In* Dve poeme. [Anabasa, i Izgnanstvo. Preveo Nikola Trajković. Kruševac, Bagdala] 1960. (Mala biblioteka) p. [21]–53.

PQ2623.E386A818   Rare Bk. Coll.

Includes translations of the prefaces by Larbaud, Hofmannsthal, and Eliot (p. 9–20) and a note on the author by the translator (p. 75–77).

These translations of the poem and the prefaces were first published in *Književnost*, g. 14, juni 1959, p. 473–493 (AP56.K63, v. 14).

SPANISH

26

Anabasis, un poema.   Traducido al castellano por Octavio G. Barreda. [México] Letras de México, 1941.   75 p.

PQ2623.E386A85   Rare Bk. Coll.

French and Spanish on opposite pages.

"Edición limitada a 300 ejemplares.   Ejemplar núm. 100."   Signed by the author.

Includes a preface by the translator (p. 7–12).

This translation and its preface were first published in *Contemporaneos*, t. 9, enero 1931, p. 1–37 (AP63.C525, v. 9), and reprinted in *Et cætera*, t. 7, enero/marzo 1961, p. 1–18 (AP63.C15, v. 7).

27

Anabasis.   Versión castellana de Jorge Zalamea Borda; ilustraciones de Giorgio de Chirico.   *In* Colombia. Universidad, *Bogotá.*   Universidad nacional de Colombia, revista trimestral de cultura moderna, no. 14, abr./mayo 1949: 57–75. plates.   AS82.B715, no. 14

An essay by Zalamea entitled "La consolacion poética," on the poetry of Saint-John Perse, appears in the same issue (p. 76–79).

28

Anabasis.   Versión, prólogo y notas de Agustín Larrauri.   [1. ed.] Madrid, Ediciones Rialp, 1957.   61 p. (Adonais, 142)

PQ2623.E386A819   1957   Rare Bk. Coll.

"Cronología de Saint-John Perse": p. 18–22.

EXIL (QUATRE POEMES)

Exil

29
Exil. [Long Beach Island, 1941] 23 leaves. mounted illus. 33 cm.
         PQ2623.E386E9 Rare Bk. Coll.
Author's holograph, signed St.-J. Perse.
Accompanied by a typewritten copy (16 leaves) and a letter from the author to Archibald MacLeish, to whom the poem is dedicated.

30
Exil. Poetry, v. 59, Mar. 1942: 295–308.   PS301.P6, v. 59
Text of poem in French.
"A Note on Alexis Saint Léger Léger," by Archibald MacLeish, and a short bibliography of the published works of Saint-John Perse appear in the same issue (p. 330–337).

31
Exil. A note on Alexis Saint Léger Léger [by] Archibald MacLeish.
[Chicago, 1942] 295–308, 330–337 p.
         PQ2623.E386E9 1942a Rare Bk. Coll.
In *Poetry,* v. 59, Mar. 1942.
"St.-J. Perse: Bibliography" (with additions in manuscript): p. 336–337.

32
Exil. Cahiers du sud, 29. année, no 246, mai 1942: 329–340.
         AP20.C163, 1942

33
Exil. Lettres françaises (Buenos Aires), 2. année, juil. 1942: 1–11.
         AP21.L4, 1942

34
Exil. Buenos Aires, Editions des Lettres françaises, 1942. [27] p.
       PQ2623.E386E9 1942 Rare Bk. Coll.
"Il a été tiré trois cent trente trois exemplaires, dont trois exemplaires hors commerce marqués A, B et C, trente exemplaires sur papier Whatman numérotés de I à XXX et trois cents exemplaires sur papier type Hollande numérotés de 1 à 300, le tout constituant l'édition originale. Exemplaire no 11."

—— Another copy. Mss
"Exemplaire no 137." Unopened. Inscribed "Au Maître de Cricket Hill et d'Alexandria, et plus simplement à Archie, affection et gratitude. Alexis St. L. L. Washington." In the Archibald MacLeish papers.

35
Exil. Neuchâtel, Editions de la Baconnière [1942] 34 p. (Les Poètes des cahiers du Rhône, 1) PQ2623.E386E9 1942b Rare Bk. Coll.

Translations

DANISH

36
Eksil. *In* Anabasis. Eksil. Overs. og med indledning af Thorkild Hansen. [København] Gyldendal, 1960. p. [73]–[100].
PQ2623.E386A813
This translation was first published in *Vindrosen,* 5. årg., jan. 1958, p. 31–41 (AP42.V53, v. 5), under the title "Landflygtighed," together with an essay by the translator entitled "Saint-John Perse og de landflygtige" (p. 18–30).

GERMAN

37
Exil. Das Lot, Bd. 3, Mai 1948: 23–32. PN6034.L6, v. 3
Translated by Leonharda Gescher.
This issue includes two essays: "Über Saint-John Perse," by Alain Bosquet, and "Über die Kunst des Dichters Saint-John Perse," by Roger Caillois (p. 7–22).

ITALIAN

38
Esilio. Fiera letteraria, anno 5, 11 giugno 1950: 3. port.
AP37.F53, v. 5
Translated by Romeo Lucchese.
This issue includes a biobibliographic note by the translator on the author (p. 4) and three articles: "Erede del simbolismo," by Liliana Magrini; "Parole chiave nel poeta di Anabase," by Raymond Marcel; and "Omaggio a Saint-John Perse," by Allen Tate (p. 3–4).

39

Rutaku. Mungen, quarterly magazine of poetry, dai 15-gō, shunki-gō 1964: 135–139.   DLC

Translated by Masaki Katayama.

This issue includes several other translations and a number of critical articles.

SERBO-CROATIAN

40

Izgnanstvo. *In* Dve poeme. [Anabasa, i Izgnanstvo. Preveo Nikola Trajković. Kruševac, Bagdala] 1960. (Mala biblioteka) p. [55]–74.

PQ2623.E386A818   Rare Bk. Coll.

Includes a note on the author by the translator (p. 75–77).

Cantos I-III of this translation were first published in *Književne novine*, g. 10, 25 sept. 1959, p. 5 (AP56.K615, 1959), and Canto IV, in the issue dated 4 nov. 1960.

SPANISH

41

Exil. Humanitas (Tucumán), no. 4, 1954: 294–311.   AS78.T82, no. 4

French and Spanish on opposite pages.

Translated by Guillermo Orce Remis.

Accompanied by a foreword by the translator (p. 291–293) and a bibliography (p. 312–314).

Poème à l'étrangère

42

Poème à l'étrangère. Hemispheres, v. 1, summer 1943: 3–7.

AP1.H4, v. 1

This issue includes an essay by Roger Caillois entitled "Sur l'art de Saint-John Perse" (p. 8–14).

43

Poème à l'étrangère. Fontaine, t. 6, no 32, 1944: 121–125.

AP27.F6, v. 6

44

Poème à l'étrangère. Nouvelle relève, v. 4, juin 1945: 81–86.

AP21.N75, v. 4

Translations

ENGLISH

45

Poème à l'étrangère.   Poem to a foreign lady.   Briarcliff quarterly, v. 2,
Jan. 1946: 214–221.   LH1.B7Q3, v. 2
French and English.
Translated by Denis Devlin.

ITALIAN

46

Poesia per la straniera.   Fiera letteraria, anno 8, 19 luglio 1953: 4.   port.
                                                   AP37.F53, v. 8
Translated by Romeo Lucchese.

Pluies

47

Pluies.   Lettres françaises (Buenos Aires), 3. année, oct. 1943: 1–9.
                                                   AP21.L4, 1943
A detached copy inscribed "Pour Archie, affectueusement, A." is in
the Archibald MacLeish papers (Mss).

48

Pluies.   Buenos Aires, Editions des Lettres françaises, 1944.   [26] p.
                        PQ2623.E386P5   1944   Rare Bk. Coll.
"De cet ouvrage . . . il a été tiré trois cent quatre-vingt douze exemplaires, dont deux exemplaires hors commerce marqués A et B, trente
exemplaires sur papier Whatman numérotés de I à XXX, trois cents
exemplaires sur papier type Hollande numérotés de 1 à 300 et soixante
exemplaires d'essai sur papier grossier dit Chandelle, le tout constituant
l'édition originale.   Exemplaire no 259."   Signed by the author.

49

Pluies.   Fontaine, t. 6, no 34, 1944: 397–405.   AP27.F6, v. 6
This issue includes an essay by Roger Caillois entitled "Sur l'art de
Saint-John Perse" (p. 406–412).

50

Pluies.   Lettres (Genève), 2. année, no 2, 1944: 5–17.   AP24.L4, v. 2

Translations

51

Rains (Pluies). The French poem with an English translation by Denis
Devlin. Sewanee, Tenn., Sewanee Review, 1945. [32] p.
                                    PQ2623.E386P5 1945 Rare Bk. Coll.
French and English on opposite pages.

"This special edition, signed by the author and the translator, is
limited to seventy-five copies, fifteen numbered I-XV, and forty [sic]
numbered 1–60. This is copy number 9."

This translation was first published in the *Sewanee Review*, v. 52,
Oct./Dec. 1944, p. 483–492 (AP2.S5, v. 52).

ITALIAN

52

Piogge. Fiera letteraria, anno 9, 24 ott. 1954: 5. port. AP37.F53, v. 9
Translated by Romeo Lucchese.

SERBO-CROATIAN

53

Kiše. [Preveo Nikola Trajković. Kruševac, Bagdala] 1962. 38 p.
(Mala biblioteka)   PQ2623.E386P518

Includes a translation, entitled "Misija pesnika," of the Nobel Prize
acceptance speech, *Poésie* (p. 9–14), and a sketch of the author by the
translator (p. 35–38).

This translation of *Pluies* was first published in *Savremenik*, g. 7,
jan. 1961, p. 62–68 (AP56.S3, v. 7), with an article, signed D. J.,
entitled "Sen Džon Pers—pesnik i moralist" (p. 69–75).

Neiges

54

Neiges. Lettres françaises (Buenos Aires), 4. année, juil. 1944: 6–10.
                                              AP21.L4, 1944

55

Neiges. Choix (London), t. 1, no 3, 1944: 41–43.   AP25.C5, v. 1

Translations

ENGLISH

56
Snows (Neiges). Translated from the French by Denis Devlin. [Sewanee, Tenn., 1945] 13 p.   PQ2623.E386N42   Rare Bk. Coll.
English and French on opposite pages.
This translation was first published in the *Sewanee Review*, v. 53, Apr./June 1945, p. 186–197 (AP2.S5, v. 53). That issue includes an essay by Roger Caillois entitled "The Art of St.-John Perse" (p. 198–206).

ITALIAN

57
Nevi. Inventario, anno 1, primavera 1946: 58–61.   AP37.I52, v. 1
Translated by Renato Poggioli.

58
Nevi. Fiera letteraria, anno 9, 21 mar. 1954: 5. port.   AP37.F53, v. 9
Translated by Romeo Lucchese.

POLISH

59
Sniegi. Znak, r. 12, grudz. 1960: 1610–1614.   AP54.Z6, v. 12
Translated by Jan Prokop.
This issue includes an article by the translator entitled "Saint-John Perse, Nobel 1960" (p. 1608–1610).

Collected Editions

60
Quatre poèmes (1941–1944). Buenos Aires, Lettres françaises, 1944. 68 p.   PQ2623.E386Q3   1944a   Rare Bk. Coll.
"Le tirage de cette édition . . . a été strictement limité à trente exemplaires sur papier Whatman numérotés de I à XXX. Exemplaire n° 22." Signed by the author.
Contents.—Exil.—Pluies.—Neiges.—Poème à l'étranger.

61

Quatre poèmes (1941–1944). Buenos Aires, Lettres françaises, Sur [1944] 76 p. (La Porte étroite, n° 7)   PQ2623.E386Q3
   Contents.—Note liminaire, par Archibald MacLeish.—Quatre poèmes: Exil. Pluies. Neiges. Poème à l'étrangère.

———— Another copy.   PQ2623.E386Q3   Rare Bk. Coll.

62

Exil, suivi de Poème à l'étrangère, Pluies, Neiges. [Paris] Gallimard [1945] 68 p. (Collection Métamorphoses, 24)
                          PQ2623.E386E9   1945   Rare Bk. Coll.
Errata leaf inserted.

63

Exil, suivi de Poèmes [sic] à l'étrangère, Pluie [sic], Neiges. [Paris] Gallimard [1946] [79] p.   PQ2623.E386E9   1946   Rare Bk. Coll.
Bibliography: p. [71]–[73].

Translations

ENGLISH

64

Exile, and other poems. Bilingual ed. Translation by Denis Devlin. [New York] Pantheon Books [1949] 166 p. (The Bollingen series, 15)   PQ2623.E386E92
Bibliography: p. [161]–166.
   In addition to the four poems, includes three essays: "The Personality of St.-John Perse," by Archibald MacLeish; "The Art of St.-John Perse," by Roger Caillois; and "The Works of St.-John Perse," by Alain Bosquet.

———— Another copy.   PQ2623.E386E92   Rare Bk. Coll.

GERMAN

65

Exil. Übertragen von Leonharda Gescher und Friedhelm Kemp. [Frankfurt a.M.] Insel-Verlag, 1961 [°1957] 62 p. (Insel-Bücherei, Nr. 730)   PQ2623.E386S94   1961   Rare Bk. Coll.
   Contents.—Exil.—Regen.—Schnee.—Gedicht an eine Fremde.—Nachwort [von] Friedhelm Kemp.

66

Lluvias. Nievas. Exilio. Versión castellana de Jorge Zalamea, ilustraciones de Luna. Milano, Italgeo [1946] 76 p. illus.

PQ2623.E386A57   Rare Bk. Coll.

"De esta edición se han impreso 500 ejemplares sobre papel Fabriano, setenticinco fuera de comercio, numerados de I a LXXV y cuatrocientos vienticinco numerados de 1 a 425. Ejemplar VI."

VENTS

67

Vents. [Paris] Gallimard [1946] [104] p.

PQ2623.E386V4   Rare Bk. Coll.

68

Winds. Bilingual ed. Translation by Hugh Chisholm. [New York] Pantheon Books [1953] 252 p. (Bollingen series, 34)

PQ2623.E386V43

Bibliography: p. [249]–252.

Includes translations of four essays: "A Poem by St.-John Perse," by Paul Claudel; "The Most Proudly Free," by Gaëtan Picon; "A Poetry Marked by Scansion," by Albert Béguin; and "St.-John Perse and Poetic Ambiguity," by Gabriel Bounoure.

Canto I of this translation was first published in the *Hudson Review,* v. 4, autumn 1951, p. 366–395 (AP2.H886, v. 4), with Chisholm's translation of the Claudel essay (p. 396–408), and Canto II, in the *Sewanee Review,* v. 60, July/Sept. 1952, p. 488–511 (AP2.S5, v. 60).

69

Winds. Translation by Hugh Chisholm. [2d] bilingual ed. [New York] Pantheon Books [1961, °1953] 193 p. (Bollingen series, 34)

PQ2623.E386V43   1961

"Bibliographical note": p. 189–193.

70

Winde. Französisch und Deutsch. Übertragung und Nachwort von

Friedhelm Kemp. [Frankfurt am Main] Suhrkamp [1964] 174 p. (Bibliothek Suhrkamp, Bd. 122)

PQ2623.E386V4   1964   Rare Bk. Coll.

French and German on opposite pages.

Part of Canto I of this translation was first published in *Merkur* (Stuttgart), 10. Jahrg., Okt. 1956, p. 973–982 (AP30.M43, v. 10).

AMERS

71

Poème.   Cahiers de la pléiade, no 4, printemps 1948: 11–12.

AP20.C146, 1948

Canto VIII of the Strophe.

72

Et vous, mers... Cahiers de la pléiade, no 10, été/automne 1950: 11–20.   AP20.C146, 1950

Cantos I–VI of the Invocation.

This special issue of *Cahiers de la pléiade,* dedicated to Saint-John Perse, includes tributes from more than 30 writers from several countries.

73

Amers.   Nouvelle nouvelle revue française, 1. année, jan.-fév. 1953: 5–26, 263–281.   AP20.N852, v. 1

Cantos I–VII of the Strophe and Cantos I–V of the Chœur.

74

Etroits sont les vaisseaux . . . Nouvelle nouvelle revue française, 4. année, juil. 1956: 1–37.   AP20.N852, v. 4

Canto IX of the Strophe.

75

Amers.   [Paris] Gallimard [1960, ᶜ1957] 187, [2] p.

PQ2623.E386A73   1960   Rare Bk. Coll.

"Note bibliographique": p. 187–[188].

76

Amers.   [Paris, Les Bibliophiles de Provence, 1962, ᶜ1957] 2 v. 20 col. illus.   PQ2623.E386A73   1962   Rare Bk. Coll.

Each vol. issued in portfolio in a case.

Vol. 2: Vingt lithographies originales inspirées à André Marchand par le thème d'Amers.

"Il a été faite . . . 250 exemplaires accompagnés de lithographies originales sur le thème d'Amers." "Exemplaire numéro 160."

Another poem, entitled "Adresse du Poète pour l'avènement d'un nouveau caractère en Imprimerie française: 'l'Italique corps 28 de Grandjean,'" is reproduced in a facsimile of the poet's manuscript in v. 1, p. [11]–[12].

Translations

ENGLISH

77
Seamarks. Translation by Wallace Fowlie. Bilingual ed. [New York] Pantheon Books [1958] 363 p. (Bollingen series, 67)

PQ2623.E386A73   1958

Bibliography: p. 359–363.
Portions of this translation were first published as follows: Cantos I–VI of the Invocation, in *Poetry,* v. 79, Oct. 1951, p. 1–22 (PS301.P6, v. 79); Cantos I–VII of the Strophe, in the *Yale Review,* v. 44, Mar. 1955, p. 389–410 (AP2.Y2, v. 44); Cantos I–V of the Chœur, in *Poetry,* v. 86, July 1955, p. 187–227 (PS301.P6, v. 86); and Canto IX of the Strophe, in *Encounter,* v. 11, Sept. 1958, p. 27–34 (AP4.E44, v. 11).

GERMAN

78
Eng sind die Schiffe. Farbradierungen von Sabine Franek-Koch. [Deutsche Übertragung von Friedhelm Kemp] Berlin, Rembrandt Verlag [1968] [7] leaves. 5 col. plates.

NE2210.F68A43   Rare Bk. Coll.

"Dieses Werk erschien . . . in zwei Ausgaben: Normalausgabe: 65 Exemplare mit Radierungen auf Büttenpapier, einzeln signiert und arabisch numeriert, in handgefertigtem Leinenband und Schuber. Luxusausgabe: 25 Exemplare mit 2 zusätzlichen, nur für diese Ausgabe geschaffenen Farbradierungen, alle auf Japanpapier, einzeln signiert und römisch numeriert, in handgefertigtem Halbpergamentband und Schuber. Den ersten fünf Exemplaren (Nr. I/XXV–V/XXV) der Luxusausgabe ist eine der Original-Zinkplatten beigefügt. Ausserdem wurden zehn nicht für den Handel bestimmte Exemplare hergestellt und mit Buchstaben (A–J) gekennzeichnet. . . . Dieses Exemplar trägt die Nummer: 34."

Translation of part of Canto IX of the Strophe, first published in *Neue Rundschau,* 68. Jahrg., 3. Heft, 1957, p. 377–407 (AP30.N5, v. 68).

79

Morekazi. [Preveo s francuskog: Borislav Radović] Beograd, Prosveta, 1963. 213 p. (Savremeni strani pisci, kolo 3., 14) PQ2623.E386A737 "Bibliografska beleška": p. 212–[214].

Includes an essay on Saint-John Perse by Miodrag Pavlović (p. 199–[204]).

SPANISH

80

Mares. [Versión castellana de Jorge Zalamea] Caracas [Dirección de Cultura Universitaria, Departamento de Publicaciones] 1961. 185 p. (Biblioteca de cultura universitaria)   PQ2623.E386A738   1961

81

Señales de mar. Versión castellana [de] Lisandro Galtier. Buenos Aires, Sur [1961] 264 p.   PQ2623.E386A73   1961   Rare Bk. Coll. Spanish and French.

This translation of the Invocation was first published in *Sur,* no. 268, enero/feb. 1961, p. 8–18 (AP63.S85, 1961), an issue which also includes a translation of Pierre Guerre's essay, "Dans la haute maison de mer: rencontres avec Saint-John Perse" (p. 18–28).

CHRONIQUE

82

Chronique. Cahiers du sud, 46. année, no 352, oct./nov. 1959: 329–343.
AP20.C163, 1959

Three essays on Saint-John Perse appear in the same issue: "Dans la haute maison de mer: rencontres avec Saint-John Perse," by Pierre Guerre; "Dans l'empire des choses vraies," by André Rousseaux; and "Quelques raisons de louer . . .," by Luc André Marcel (p. 344–376).

83

Chronique. [Marseille, Presses de la Sopic, 1959] 58 p. port. DLC "Le present tirage à part du numéro 352 des Cahiers du sud comprenant la première impression du poème de Saint-John Perse: Chronique est limité à cent exemplaires hors commerce numérotés de 1 à 100 sur papier pur fil Lafuma et quelques exemplaires nominatifs destinés aux amis de l'auteur et de la revue. Exemplaire N° 16."

Includes the three essays cited in the preceding item (p. 25–58).

84
Chronique. [Paris] Gallimard [1960] 30 p.   4PQ Fr–3669

Translations

BENGALI

85
Bṛttānta. Anubādaka: Pṛthvīndranātha Mukhopādhyāẏa. Kataka, Pra-
phullacandra Dāsa [1960] 44 p. port.   DLC

Includes a translation, "Syām̐-jan Pyārsera Bhāshaṇa," of the Nobel Prize acceptance speech, *Poésie* (p. 14–19).

ENGLISH

86
Chronique. Translation by Robert Fitzgerald. Bilingual ed. [New York] Pantheon Books [1961] 60 p. (Bollingen series, 69)
                               PQ2623.E386C43   Rare Bk. Coll.
Bibliography: p. [49]–60.

GERMAN

87
Chronik. Merkur (Stuttgart), 14. Jahrg., Nov. 1960: 1037–1047.
                               AP30.M43, v. 14
Translated by Friedhelm Kemp.

SPANISH

88
Crónica. Poesia española, 2. época, no. 95, nov. 1960: 10–15.
                               PQ6187.P58, 1960
Translated by Manuel Alvarez Ortega.

This special issue, dedicated to Saint-John Perse, includes translations of extracts from "Amitié du prince" and *Exil*, a bibliography, a chronology, an essay by José Gerardo Manrique de Lara entitled "Mundo poetico de Saint-John Perse," and some miscellaneous writings about the poet excerpted from other publications.

89

Crónica. Revista nacional de cultura (Caracas), año 23, enero/feb. 1961: 49–59.   AS90.A1R4, 1961
    Translated by Guillermo Sucre.

90

Crónica. Versión castellana de Lysandro Z. D. Galtier. Buenos Aires, Compañía General Fabril [°1961] 56 p. port. (Los Poetas)   DLC
    Includes a translation of the Nobel Prize acceptance speech, *Poésie* (p. 13–21).

OISEAUX

91

L'Ordre des oiseaux [par] Georges Braque [et] Saint-John Perse. [Paris] Au vent d'Arles, 1962. 48 p. 12 col. illus.
                     PQ2623.E386O7   Rosenwald Coll.
    "L'édition originale de L'Ordre des oiseaux a été à cent trente exemplaires . . . accompagnés d'une suite des eaux-fortes signées et numérotées par l'artiste, et cent exemplaires numérotés de 1 à 100 signés par les auteurs . . . Exemplaire 67."

92

Oiseaux. Nouvelle revue française, 10. année, déc. 1962: 969–987.
                     AP20.N852, v. 10

93

Oiseaux. [Paris] Gallimard [1963] 33 p.   PQ2623.E386O7   1963

Translations

ENGLISH

94

Birds [by] St.-John Perse [and] Georges Braque. Portfolio, no. 7, winter 1963: 25–31, 117–120. 4 col. illus.   N1.P82, no. 7
    French and English in parallel columns.
    Translated by Wallace Fowlie.
    A short, unsigned introduction, with small portraits of poet and painter, appears on p. 24.

Birds. With reproductions of four original color etchings by Georges Braque. Translation by Robert Fitzgerald. Bilingual ed. [New York] Pantheon Books [1966] 71 p. 4 col. plates. (Bollingen series, 82)

PQ2623.E386O7   1966

"Bibliographical note": p. [65]–71.

–––– Another copy.   PQ2623.E386O7   1966   Rare Bk. Coll.

96

Birds. Translated by J. Roger Little. Durham [North Gate Press] 1967. 17 p.   PQ2623.E386O73

Limited edition of 103 copies.

GERMAN

97

Oiseaux. Vögel. [Aus dem Französischen übertragen von Friedhelm Kemp. Neuwied] Luchterhand [1964] 61 p. col. illus. (on lining papers)   PQ2623.E386O7   1964   Rare Bk. Coll.

French and German on opposite pages.

Two of the Braque etchings are reproduced.

This translation was first published in *Jahresring* 63/64, p. 63–75 (Stuttgart, Deutsche Verlags–Anstalt [ᶜ1963] PT1141.J3, 63/64).

COLLECTIONS

98

Œuvre poétique. 1. [Paris] Gallimard [1953] 477 p.

PQ2623.E386A6   1953

"Index bibliographique": p. [449]–468.

Contents.—Eloges.—La gloire des rois.—Anabase.—Exil.—Vents.

99

Œuvre poétique. Ed rev. et corr. [Paris] Gallimard [1960] 2 v. (Collection Soleil, 52–53)   PQ2623.E386A6   1960

"Index bibliographique": v. 1, p. [235]–[244]; v. 2, p. [345]–[351].

Contents.—1. Eloges. La gloire des rois. Anabase. Exil.—2. Vents. Amers. Chronique.

100

Saint-John Perse. Présentation par Alain Bosquet. Choix de textes, bibliographie, dessins, portraits, fac-similés. [Paris] P. Seghers [1953]

207 p. illus., facsims., map, ports. (Poètes d'aujourd'hui, 35)

PQ2623.E386S3

Bibliography: p. 185–204.

101

Saint-John Perse. Présentation par Alain Bosquet. Choix de textes, bibliographie, dessins, portraits, fac-similés. Ed. rev. et augm. [Paris] P. Seghers [1964] 208 p. illus., facsims., map, ports. (Poètes d'aujourd'hui, 35) PQ2623.E386A6 1964
Bibliography: p. 199–[206].

102

Saint-John Perse. Présentation par Alain Bosquet. Choix de textes, bibliographie, dessins, portraits, fac-similés. Ed. rev. et augm. [Paris] P. Seghers [1967] 190 p. illus., facsims., map, ports. (Poètes d'aujourd'hui, 35) PQ2623.E386A6 1967
Bibliography: p. 180–187.

103

Eloges. Suivi de La gloire des rois, Anabase, Exil. [Paris] Gallimard [1967] 221 p. (Collection Poésie) PQ2623.E386E32

104

Vents. Suivi de Chronique. [Paris] Gallimard [1968] 157 p. (Collection Poésie, v. 36) PQ2623.E386V4 1968

105

Amers. Suivi de Oiseaux et de Poésie. [Paris] Gallimard [1970] 255 p. (Collection Poésie, 53) PQ2623.E386A73 1970

Translations

CZECH

106

Vichry. [Z francouzských originálů vybrali Jiří Kolář a Bohumila Grögerova] Přel. Jiří Kolář, Bohumila Grögerová a Jiří Konůpek. [Vyd. 1.] Praha, Státní nakl. krásné literatury a umění, 1965. 147 p. port. (Plamen, Edice současné zahraniční poezie, sv. 45)

PQ2623.E386V42

Contents.—Obrazy pro Crusoa.—Anabaze.—Exil.—Deště.—Sněhy.—Báseň cizince.—Vichry.

Includes a translation of Louis Aragon's essay on Saint-John Perse,

" 'Car c'est de l'homme qu'il s'agit...,' " and an unsigned biographical note (p. 136–147).

GERMAN

107
Dichtungen. Französisch und Deutsch. Hrsg. von Friedhelm Kemp. [Die deutsche Ausg. besorgte Friedhelm Kemp unter Benutzung der Übertragungen von Walter Benjamin, Bernard Groethuysen, Rudolf Kassner, Leonharda Gescher, Herbert Steiner] Mit Texten von Valery Larbaud [u.a. Darmstadt] H. Luchterhand [1957] 463 p.
                    PQ2623.E386A6   1957   Rare Bk. Coll.
French and German on opposite pages.
Bibliography: p. [443]–452.
Contents.—Eloges. Preislieder.—La gloire des rois. Der Ruhm der Könige.—Anabase. Anabasis.—Exil. Exil.—Vents. Winde.
Includes the prefaces to Anabase by Valery Larbaud, Hugo von Hofmannsthal, and T. S. Eliot, Paul Claudel's essay on *Vents,* an essay on Saint-John Perse by Alain Bosquet, and notes by the editor, all in German.

ITALIAN

108
Opere poetiche. Milano, Lerici [1960-65] 2 v. facsims., ports. (Poeti europei, 5, 20)   PQ2623.E386A6   1960b   Rare Bk. Coll.
French and Italian on opposite pages.
Translations by Romeo Lucchese and Giuseppe Ungaretti.
Contents.—v. 1. Elogi (Eloges). La gloria dei re (La gloire des rois). Anabasi (Anabase). Esilio (Exil).—v. 2. Venti (Vents). Cronaca (Chronique). Uccelli (Oiseaux).
Includes an introductory essay by Romeo Lucchese and a biographical sketch of the author.

SPANISH

109
Antología poética. Selección, traducción y prólogo de Jorge Zalamea. Buenos Aires, Compañía General Fabril [1960] 174 p. port. (Los Poetas)
                              PQ2623.E386A87
Contents.—Elogios: Para celebrar una infancia. Amistad del príncipe. Imágenes para Crusoe.—Anabasis.—Lluvia.—Nieve.—Exilio.—Vientos: Canto 3.—Mares: Estrechos son los bajeles.

PROSE AND SHORTER
POETICAL WRITINGS

1911

110

[Extraits de deux lettres à André Gide] Cahiers de la pléiade, no 10, été/automne 1950: 25–26.   AP20.C146, 1950

Dating from April 1911 and signed A. S. L., these excerpts are quoted by Gide in an article entitled "Don d'un arbre," contributed to this special issue honoring Saint-John Perse.

1922

111

Poème, pour M. Valery Larbaud.   Cahiers de la pléiade, no 10, été/automne 1950: 153–154.   AP20.C146, 1950

First published in *Intentions,* nov. 1922 (not in LC), a special issue dedicated to Larbaud.

112

[German translation] Poème, pour M. Valery Larbaud. Gedicht. Neue Rundschau, 72. Jahrg., 2. Heft, 1961: 268–271.   AP30.N5, v. 72

French and German on opposite pages.   Translated by Friedhelm Kemp.

1924

113

Aumône aux hommes de peu de poids. Commerce (Paris), no 3, hiver 1924: 11.   AP20.C56, v. 1

Adaptation of "A Penny for the Old Guy," part of "The Hollow Men," by T. S. Eliot.

1925

114

Lettre sur Jacques Rivière. Nouvelle revue française, t. 24, avril 1925: 455–462.   AP20.N85, v. 24

Signed A. Saint-Léger Léger. This is a special issue dedicated to Rivière.

1941

115

Fragments d'une lettre privée de Saint-John Perse à Archibald MacLeish (1942). Cahiers de la pléiade, no 10, été/automne 1950: 155–156.

AP20.C146, 1950

Holograph of letter, in the Archibald MacLeish papers (Mss), is dated 23 déc. 1941 (see item 200).

116

[English translation. Excerpts from a letter to Archibald MacLeish] Poetry, v. 59, Mar. 1942: 334–336. PS301.P6, v. 59

Quoted by MacLeish in his article, "A Note on Alexis Saint Léger Léger," accompanying the first publication of *Exil* (see items 30 and 31).

1948

117

Extrait d'une lettre à Max-Pol Fouchet. *In* Honneur à Saint-John Perse, hommages et témoignages littéraires. [Paris] Gallimard [1965] p. 654.

PQ2623.E386Z715

Fragment.

1949

118

[Lettre à Octavio Barreda] Et cætera, t. 7, enero/marzo 1961: [16a]–[16d]. AP63.C15, v. 7

Facsimile of a letter dated 6 nov. 1949. Accompanies a reprinting of Barreda's translation of *Anabase* (see item 26).

1950

119

[Extrait d'une lettre à Paul Claudel] *In* Claudel, Paul. Œuvres en prose. Préface par Gaëtan Picon. Textes établis et annotés par Jacques Petit et Charles Galpérine. [Paris, Gallimard, 1965] (Bibliothèque de la pléiade, 179) p. 1482–1483. PQ2605.L2A13

Dated 7 jan. 1950. Expresses appreciation for Claudel's essay, "Un poème de Saint-John Perse," published in *Revue de Paris,* 56. année, nov. 1949, p. 3–15 (AP20.R27, v. 56).

120

Réponse à une allocution américaine (1950). Cahiers de la pléiade, no 10, été/automne 1950: 157.   AP20.C146, 1950

A brief address in response to the presentation, by Archibald Mac-
Leish on behalf of the American Academy of Arts and Letters, of the
Award of Merit Medal for Poetry.   This text omits the short final para-
graph published in the following item.

121

[English translation] Acceptance. *In* American Academy of Arts and
Letters. Proceedings, ser. 2, no. 1; 1950. New York, 1951. p. 21–23.
                                                   AS36.A47, s. 2, no. 1
French and English. Translated by Archibald MacLeish.

1951

122

Face aux lettres françaises, 1909. *In* La Nouvelle revue française.
Hommage à André Gide, 1869–1951; hommages de l'étranger; Gide
dans les lettres; André Gide tel que je l'ai vu; textes inédits.   Paris
[Gallimard] 1951. (La Nouvelle revue française, nov. 1951) p. 75–86.
                                                   PQ2613.I2Z6564
Dated Washington, 29 mai 1951.

123

[English translation] Andre Gide: 1909. Sewanee review, v. 60, Oct./
Dec. 1952: 593–604.   AP2.S5, v. 60
Translated by Mina Curtiss.

124

[Swedish translation] Gide och den franska litteraturen. BLM, Bonniers litterära magasin, årg. 29, dec. 1960: 819–825.   AP48.B6, v. 29
Translated by Ingemar Gustafson.

125

[Lettre à Francis de Miomandre] *In* Honneur à Saint-John Perse, hommages et témoignages littéraires.   [Paris] Gallimard [1965] p. 636–
637.   PQ2623.E386Z715
Dated Washington, 7 juin 1951.   Declines an invitation to become
a candidate for election to the Académie Mallarmé.

126

Message pour Valery Larbaud. Cahiers de la pléiade, no 13, automne
1951/printemps 1952: 11–14.   AP20.C146, 1952
Dated Boston, août 1951.

127

[German translation] Botschaft für Valery Larbaud. Neue Rundschau, 68. Jahrg., 2. Heft, 1957: 220–223.   AP30.N5, v. 68
    Translated by Friedhelm Kemp.

1953

128

[Lettre à Roger Caillois] *In* Caillois, Roger. Poétique de St.-John Perse. [Paris] Gallimard [1954] p. 180–181.   PQ2623.E386Z65
    Dated 26 jan. 1953.

129

Poète, Schehadé. *In* Compagnie Madeleine Renaud—Jean Louis Barrault. Cahiers, no 4, 1954: 23.   PN2635.C58, 1954
    Dated Washington, déc. 1953. A facsimile of the last few lines of the manuscript appears on p. 24.

1955

130

To the editors of "Poetry." Poetry, v. 86, June 1955: [i].

PS301.P6, v. 86
    Letter dated Washington, 24 fév. 1955. In French. An appeal for donations in support of *Poetry* magazine.

131

Silence pour Claudel. Nouvelle nouvelle revue française, 3. année, sept. 1955: 387–391.   AP20.N852, v. 3
    Dated Mer Caraïbe au large de Saba, 4 mars 1955.

1956

132

Pour Adrienne Monnier. Mercure de France, t. 326, jan. 1956: 11–12.
    AP20.M5, v. 326
    A special issue dedicated to Adrienne Monnier. This tribute is reprinted in her *Rue de l'Odéon,* p. [9]–10 (Paris, A. Michel [1960] Z1003.M73).

133

Une lettre de Saint-John Perse. A letter from Saint-John Perse. [To George Huppert] Berkeley review, no. 1, winter 1956: 34–41.
    PS508.C6B44, 1956

Dated Tenant's Harbor, Maine, 10 août 1956.   French and English on opposite pages.   Translated by Arthur J. Knodel.

This first issue of the *Berkeley Review* is dedicated to Saint-John Perse and contains articles by Knodel, René Girard, and Huppert, as well as fragments of Canto IX of the Strophe of *Amers,* with English translations by Huppert.

The French text of the letter is reprinted as "Une lettre de Saint-John Perse sur l'expression poétique française" in *Biblio,* 27. année, jan. 1959, p. 7–8 (Z2165.B56, v. 27).

1957

134

Larbaud; ou, L'honneur littéraire.   Nouvelle revue française, 5. année, sept. 1957: 387–400.   AP20.N852, v. 5

A special issue devoted to Valery Larbaud.

1958

135

Message pour Giuseppe Ungaretti.   *In* Ungaretti, Giuseppe.   Il taccuino del vecchio; con testimonianze di amici stranieri del poeta raccolte a cura di Leone Piccioni e una scritto introduttivo di Jean Paulhan.   [Milano] A. Mondadori [1960] p. 103.   4PQ It. 3424

Dated Washington, 10 fév. 1958.   Reprinted in *Ungaretti,* p. 297 ([Paris, Editions de L'Herne, 1968?] L'Herne.   Cahier no 11. PQ4845. N4Z9).

1959

136

La thematique d'Amers.   Tematiken i Amers.   BLM, Bonniers litterära magasin, årg. 28, jan. 1959: 26–29.   AP48.B6, v. 28

French and Swedish on opposite pages.   Translated by Erik Lindegren.

The French text was reprinted as "Les thèmes d'Amers" in *Nouvelle revue française,* 7. année, avril 1959, p. 734–736 (AP20.N852, v. 7).

137

Réponse [à une allocution de M. André Malraux] *In* Honneur à Saint-John Perse, hommages et témoignages littéraires.   [Paris] Gallimard [1965] p. 640.   PQ2623.E386Z715

Acceptance of the Grand prix national des lettres, presented on Nov. 9, 1959.

1960

138

Extrait d'une lettre à Dag Hammarskjöld. *In* Honneur à Saint-John Perse, hommages et témoignages littéraires. [Paris] Gallimard [1965] p. 667.   PQ2623.E386Z715

Fragment on the significance of the title *Chronique*, first published in the Swedish bilingual edition *Chronique; Krönika* ([Stockholm] Bonnier [1960] 48 p. not in LC).

139

Garde, ô passion! *In* Honneur à Saint-John Perse, hommages et témoignages littéraires. [Paris] Gallimard [1965] p. [808a]

PQ2623.E386Z715

Facsimile of a quatrain based on the inscription of a 17th-century Zen painting (also reproduced and translated), from the collection of Hugues Le Gallais. Copied from an exhibition catalog entitled *Raccolta d'arte orientale* (Venezia, Studio del Tiziano [1960?] 172 p. not in LC).

140

Lettre à M. Pierre Béarn. *In* Honneur à Saint-John Perse, hommages et témoignages littéraires. [Paris] Gallimard [1965] p. 667.

PQ2623.E386Z715

Dated Presqu'île de Giens, 9 oct. 1960. Refuses designation as "Prince des Poètes."

141

[Poésie] Allocution de Saint-John Perse au Banquet Nobel, 10 Décembre 1960. 4 leaves. 27 cm.   Mss

Typescript (carbon copy) with emendations in an unknown hand. Dated by the author and inscribed "Pour *vous,* cher Mondor, très amicalement. A. L."

In the Alexis Leger papers, Miscellaneous Manuscript Collection.

142

[Poésie] Allocution de Stockholm. Cahiers du sud, 48. année, no 358, déc. 1960/jan. 1961: 375–380.   AP20.C163, 1961

The Nobel Prize acceptance speech, delivered in Stockholm on Dec. 10, 1960. The full text appeared in the report "Saint-John Perse reçoit à Stockholm le Prix Nobel de littérature," published in *Le Monde,* 17. année, 11/12 déc. 1960, p. 16 (N&CPR), and in other Paris papers.

143

Poésie. Nouvelle revue française, 9. année, jan. 1961: 79–84.

AP20.N852, v. 9

144
Poésie; allocution au banquet Nobel du 10 décembre 1960. [Paris]
Gallimard [1961] [11] p.   PN1031.L38

145
[Bengali translation] Syām-jan Pyārsera Bhāshana. *In his* Bṛttānta.
Anubādaka: Pṛthvīndranātha Mukhopādhyāẏa. Kataka, Praphullacan-
dra Dāsa [1960] p. 14–19.   DLC

146
[English translation] On poetry, speech of acceptance upon the award
of the Nobel prize for literature. Delivered in Stockholm, December
10, 1960. Translated by W. H. Auden. With the French text. [New
York, Bollingen Foundation, ʿ1961] 21 p. (Bollingen series)
                                                    PN1031.L38   1961
    "Works of St.-John Perse published, with English translations, in the
United States of America": p. 21–[22].
    This translation appeared as "The Poet as 'Guilty Conscience of His
Time'" in the *Washington Post,* Jan. 22, 1961, p. E–1 (N&CPR).

147
[English translation] On poetry. Translated by W. H. Auden. *In his*
Two addresses. [New York] Pantheon Books [1966] (Bollingen
series, 86) p. 9–14, 37–42.   PN1031.L383
    English and French.
    "Works of St.-John Perse published, with English translations, in the
United States of America": p. 61–62.

148
[German translation] Ansprache in Stockholm am 10. Dezember 1960.
Neue Rundschau, 71. Jahrg., 4. Heft, 1960: 567–570.   AP30.N5, v. 71
    Translated by Friedhelm Kemp. This translation appeared as "Das
Licht der Poesie" in the *Süddeutsche Zeitung* (Munich), 16. Jahrg.,
17./18. Dez. 1960, p. 47 (N&CPR).

149
[Japanese translation] Shi. Mungen, quarterly magazine of poetry, dai
15–gō, shunki–gō 1964: 144–146. port.   DLC
    Translated by Komao Naruse.

150
[Serbo-Croatian translation] Misija pesnika. *In his* Kiše. [Preveo
Nikola Trajković. Kruševac, Bagdala] 1962. (Mala biblioteka) p. 9–
14.   PQ2623.E386P518

151

[Spanish translation] Poesía. *In his* Crónica. Versión castellana de Lysandro Z. D. Galtier. Buenos Aires, Compañía General Fabril [ᶜ1961] p. 13–21.   DLC

Other versions appeared in periodicals as follows: "El poeta en nuestro mundo," translated by Rómulo Sagasta, in *Sur,* no. 269, marzo/abr. 1961, p. 1–4 (AP63.S85, 1961); "Poesía," in *La Torre,* año 9, abr./jun. 1961, p. 11–15 (AS74.A1T6, 1961); and "Elogio de la poesía," translated by Sira Jaén, in *Revista de filosofía de la Universidad de Costa Rica,* v. 3, jul./dic. 1961, p. 179–181 (B5.R413, v. 3).

152

[Swedish translation] Tal vid Nobelfesten den 10 december 1960. BLM, Bonniers litterära magasin, årg. 30, jan. 1961: 24–26.

AP48.B6, v. 30

Translated by Malou Höjer.

1961

153

Adresse du poète pour l'avènement d'un nouveau caractère en imprimerie française: "l'italique corps 28 de Grandjean." *In his* Amers. [v. 1.   Paris, Les Bibliophiles de Provence, 1962, ᶜ1957] p. [11]–[12].

PQ2623.E386A73   1962   v. 1   Rare Bk. Coll.

Dated Presqu'île de Giens, été 1961.   Facsimile of the manuscript.

154

Hommage à la mémoire de Rabindranath Tagore.   Nouvelle revue française, 9. année, nov. 1961: 868–871.   AP20.N852, v. 9

Reprinted in *Hommage de la France à Rabindranath Tagore pour le centenaire de sa naissance, 1961,* p. 9–[11] (Paris, Institut de civilisation indienne, 1962.   PK1725.C65), issued by the Comité national pour la célébration du centenaire de la naissance de Rabindranath Tagore.

1962

155

Carta de Saint John Perse [a Robert Richman]   Sur, no. 276, mayo/jun. 1962: 72.   AP63.S85, 1962

In Spanish.   A tribute to Jorge Luis Borges, read at a dinner given in his honor in Washington, Feb. 19, 1962.

1963

156

Léon-Paul Fargue, poète. Nouvelle revue française, 11. année, août-sept. 1963: 197–210, 406–422. AP20.N852, v. 11

Reprinted in Fargue's *Poésies,* p. 7–31 ([Paris] Gallimard [1963] PQ2611.A66P65 1963).

157

A ceux des Cahiers du sud. Cahiers du sud, 50. année, no 373/374, sept./nov. 1963: 3–5. AP20.C163, 1963

Dated sept. 1963. Celebrates the 50th anniversary of *Cahiers du sud.*

158

A ceux des Cahiers du sud. [Marseille, 1963] 4 p. PQ2623.E386A62

"Cent exemplaires tirés à part du no double 373–374 des Cahiers du sud, septembre-novembre 1963. No 56."

159

Grandeur de Kennedy. Le Monde, 20. année, 26 nov. 1963: 1. N&CPR

A detached copy, accompanied by a letter from Mme Leger, is in the Huntington Cairns papers (Mss).

160

[English translation. Kennedy] *In* Salinger, Pierre, *and* Sander Vanocur, *eds.* A tribute to John F. Kennedy. Chicago, Encyclopaedia Britannica [1964] p. 78–79. E842.S28

1964

161

Sacre d'un deuil. Vogue, v. 143, Feb. 1, 1964: 144–145.

TT500.V7, v. 143

In honor of Jacqueline Kennedy.

162

"Pierre levée." Derrière le miroir, no 144/146, mai 1964: 5.

N2.D4, 1964

A special issue dedicated to Georges Braque.

1965

163

Pour Dante. [Paris] Gallimard [1965] 20 p. PQ4341.L43

Also published in v. 2 of the *Atti* del Congresso internazionale di studi dantesche, p. [21]–29 (PQ4363.B65C55, v. 2).

164

[English translation] Dante. Translated by Robert Fitzgerald. *In his*
Two addresses. [New York] Pantheon Books [1966] (Bollingen
series, 86) p. 17–31, 45–58. PN1031.L383
English and French.
"Works of St.-John Perse published, with English translations, in the
United States of America": p. 61–62.

165

[German translation] Für Dante. Rede zur Eröffnung des Internatio-
nalen Kongresses anlässlich der Siebenhundertjahr-Feier von Dantes Ge-
burtstag, Florenz, den 20. April 1965. *In* Jahresring, 66/67. Stuttgart,
Deutsche Verlags-Anstalt [ᶜ1966] p. 255–266. PT1141.J3, 66/67
Translated by Friedhelm Kemp.

1969

166

Chanté par celle qui fut là. Nouvelle revue française, 17. année, jan.
1969: 1–5. AP20.N852, v. 17

166a

[English translation] Chanté par celle qùi fut là... Translation by
Richard Howard. [Princeton, N.J.] Princeton University Press, 1970.
[15] p. PQ2623.E386C4
English and French.

167

Alain Bosquet en notre temps. Marginales, 24. année, avril 1969: 3.
AP22.M34, 1969

WRITINGS OF ALEXIS LEGER

1917

168

Une lettre privée d'Alexis Leger à son ministre en Chine, Alexandre
Conty; compte rendu d'une mission locale, Pékin, juillet 1917: "Relation
respectueuse." *In* Honneur à Saint-John Perse, hommages et témoi-
gnages littéraires. [Paris] Gallimard [1965] p. 687–690.
PQ2623.E386Z715
An entertaining account describing the removal of the family of
President Li Yüan-hung to a place of safety in the legation quarter of
Peking during a coup d'état which briefly restored the Manchu dynasty.

1927

169

Discours de M. Aristide Briand, Député, Ministre des affaires étrangères, prononcé au banquet de clôture de la conférence, à la Salle Wagram, mardi soir, 30 août 1927. *In* Inter-Parliamentary Union. La France et l'œuvre interparlementaire; discours prononcés à la XXIVe conférence de l'Union. Lausanne, Payot, 1927. p. 18–24.   JX1730.I71A5 1927
A somewhat different text, with attribution to Leger, appears in *Honneur à Saint-John Perse*, p. 753–758.

1928

170

Discours de M. Aristide Briand, Ministre des affaires étrangères, à la signature du Pacte générale de renonciation à la guerre, le 27 août 1928. *In* France. *Ministère des affaires étrangères.* Pacte générale de renonciation à la guerre comme instrument de politique nationale. Trente pièces relatives à la préparation, à l'élaboration et à la conclusion du Traité signé à Paris le 27 août 1928. Paris, Impr. des Journaux officiels, 1928. p. 56–59.   JX1987.A4 1928p
A shortened text, with attribution to Leger, appears in *Honneur à Saint-John Perse*, p. 695–697. The two principal articles of the pact, also attributed to Leger, appear on p. 55 and p. 697, respectively.

171

[English translation] Text of M. Briand's address to the plenipotentiaries before signing of the Pact for the Renunciation of War, August 27, 1928. *In* Shotwell, James T. The pact of Paris, with historical commentary. Text of treaty and related documents. Worcester, Mass., Carnegie Endowment for International Peace, Division of Intercourse and Education [1928] (International conciliation, Oct. 1928. no. 243) p. 80–84.   JX1908.A8, no. 243
Reprinted from the *New York Times,* Aug. 28, 1928. Articles 1 and 2 of the pact appear on p. 86–87.

172

[English translation] Address by M. Aristide Briand, French Minister for Foreign Affairs. *In* Renunciation of War Treaty, *Paris, Aug. 27, 1928.* Treaty for the renunciation of war. Text of the treaty, notes exchanged, instruments of ratification and of adherence, and other papers. Washington, U.S. Govt. Print. Off., 1933. ([U.S.] Dept. of State. Publication no. 468) p. 307–315. JX1987.A4 1928n French and English. This translation, which differs from that given in the preceding item, was probably made at the Department of State. French and English texts of articles 1 and 2 of the treaty appear on p. 4.

1930

173
Memorandum sur l'organisation d'un régime d'union fédérale européenne. [Paris, 1930] 16 p. D443.F7 1930b
Issued by the Ministère des affaires étrangères. The same text also appears in its *Documents relatifs à l'organisation d'un régime d'union fédérale européenne*, p. [9]–21 ([Paris? 1930] D443.F7 1930). First attributed to Leger and reprinted in *Cahiers de la pléiade,* no 10, été/automne 1950, p. 166–177 (AP20.C146, 1950).

174
[English translation] Memorandum on the organization of a régime of European federal union, addressed to twenty-six governments of Europe, by M. Briand, Foreign Minister of France, May 17, 1930. Worcester, Mass., Carnegie Endowment for International Peace, Division of Intercourse and Education [1930] 33 p. (International conciliation. Special bulletin, June 1930) D443.F7 1930ba
French and English on opposite pages. Translation made in the U.S. Department of State.

175
[English translation] Memorandum on the organisation of a system of European federal union. *In* France. *Ministère des affaires étrangères.* Documents relating to the organization of a system of European federal union. [Geneva, 1930] (League of Nations publications. VII, political. 1930, VII, 4) p. 9–13. D443.F7 1930a
Distributed to the Council, the members of the League, and the delegates at the Assembly.
This translation, which varies from that in the preceding entry, appears to be identical with one published earlier in a *Despatch to His Majesty's Ambassador in Paris Enclosing the Memorandum of the French Government on the Organisation of a System of European Federal Union* (London, H. M. Stationery Off., 1930. 25 p. [Gt. Brit. Parliament. Papers by command] Cmd. 3595. D443.F7 1930c).

1935

176

Une enquête sur l'optimisme: réponse d'Alexis Leger au journal Excelsior, 27 février 1935. *In* Honneur à Saint-John Perse, hommages et témoignages littéraires. [Paris] Gallimard [1965] p. 783.

PQ2623.E386Z715

177

[Extrait d'une lettre à Edouard Herriot] *In* Soulié, Michel. La vie politique d'Edouard Herriot. [Paris] A. Colin, 1962. p. 467.

DC373.H4S6

Dates from late October 1935. Congratulates Herriot on his speech, made at a congress of the Radical Party, in support of the League of Nations during the Abyssinian crisis.

1940

178

Lettre au Président Edouard Herriot. *In* Honneur à Saint-John Perse, hommages et témoignages littéraires. [Paris] Gallimard [1965] p. 713–714.

PQ2623.E386Z715

Dated Arcachon, 28 mai 1940. Describes the base manner of his summary dismissal from the post of Secretary General of the Ministry of Foreign Affairs and explains his actions. Herriot's reply appears on p. 715.

1942

179

Briand. [Aurora, N.Y., Printed by V. & J. Hammer, Wells College Press, 1943] 20 p. (Aurora, 3)

DC373.B7L4

"One hundred and fifty copies."

An address given, in French, at New York University, Mar. 28, 1942.

—— Another copy.

DC373.B7L4   Rare Bk. Coll.

180

[English translation] Aristide Briand. *In* New York University. Addresses in commemoration of the eightieth anniversary of the birth of Aristide Briand, honorary alumnus and far-seeing champion of European federation and international peace. New York [1942] p. 8–17.

DC373.B7N4   Rare Bk. Coll.

181

[German translation] Rede auf Briand. Rheinischer Merkur (Cologne), 15. Jahrg., 4 Nov. 1960: 7–8. N&CPR

Translated by Dr. Jakob Laubach.

182

Réponse d'Alexis Leger au Général de Gaulle. *In* Honneur à Saint-John Perse, hommages et témoignages littéraires. [Paris] Gallimard [1965] p. 727–728. PQ2623.E386Z715

Dated Washington, 25 mai 1942. Declines General de Gaulle's invitation of May 18 (printed on p. 727) to join the Free French National Committee in London. De Gaulle's response (conveyed through Adrien Tixier) indicating that the letter of May 18 did not come from him, appears on p. 728.

183

14 juillet 1942: an III de l'exil. Pour la victoire, v. 1, 18 juil. 1942: 2. DC334.V5, v. 1

A draft (typescript unsigned) is in the Central Files (CS).

184

Réponse de M. Alexis Leger [au télégramme de M. Winston Churchill] *In* Honneur à Saint-John Perse, hommages et témoignages littéraires. [Paris] Gallimard [1965] p. 729. PQ2623.E386Z715

Sent July 26, 1942, by the British Ambassador in Washington. Despite an appeal from Churchill, whose telegram of June 17 urging reconsideration is given on p. 728, maintains his decision not to join the Free French National Committee.

1943

185

Lettre au Président Roosevelt sur le maintien des Etats-Unis dans un politique de securité collective. *In* Honneur à Saint-John Perse, hommages et témoignages littéraires. [Paris] Gallimard [1965] p. 730. PQ2623.E386Z715

Dated Washington, 3 nov. 1943. Comments on the hopes for peace through world organization aroused by the achievements of the Moscow Conference and on the future relationships of France with Europe and the United States. President Roosevelt's acknowledgment appears on p. 731.

186

A selection of works for an understanding of world affairs since 1914.

Washington, 1943.   87 p.   Z6264.L5
At head of title: The Library of Congress.   Division of Bibliography.

1944

187
La production littéraire en France depuis la guerre, choix bibliographique
restreint.   [n.p., 1944?]   [37] leaves.   Z2161.L5
Photocopy (negative) of holograph.

188
Foreword.   *In* U.S. *Library of Congress. General Reference and Bibliography Division.*   France: a list of references on contemporary economic, social and political conditions, compiled by Helen F. Conover.
Washington, 1944.   p. [iii]–[v].   Z7165.F8U5

1945

189
La publication française pendant la guerre, bibliographie restreinte
(1940–1945).   [n.p., 1945?]   4 v.   Z2161.L52
Holograph; all but six leaves of v. 1 in Leger's hand.
Contents.—[1] Introduction.   Convention sur la censure des livres.
1940.—[2] 1941.—[3] 1942.—[4] 1943.
The introduction includes some observations on intellectual activity
—writing in particular—in wartime France.

——— v. 1, incomplete.   [71] leaves.   Z2161.L522
Photocopy (negative).   Lacks the introductory matter but includes a
photocopy of Leger's letter of Apr. 23, 1945, transmitting the bibliography to Verner Clapp for use in acquisitions.

190
Lettre à Léon Blum.   *In* Honneur à Saint-John Perse, hommages et
témoignages littéraires.   [Paris] Gallimard [1965] p. 731.
                                        PQ2623.E386Z715
Dated Washington, 28 sept. 1945.

1955

191
Réponse à un historien allemand sur l'attitude d'Alexis Leger à l'égard
des réfugiés français et des autorités britanniques, à Londres, en juin
1940.   *In* Honneur à Saint-John Perse, hommages et témoignages littéraires.   [Paris] Gallimard [1965] p. 725–726.   PQ2623.E386Z715
Dated Washington, 15 sept. 1955.   To Dr. Klaus-Jürgen Müller.

192

Letter, 1940 Oct. 18, New York, N.Y., to [Archibald MacLeish, Washington, D.C.] [6] p. on 3 leaves. 24 cm.   Mss
    Holograph signed Alexis St. L. Leger.
    In the Archibald MacLeish papers.

A response to two letters, thanking MacLeish for his friendly and tactful solicitude. Leger is awaiting the outcome of the Riom trial for its possible effects on his freedom of action. "A dire aussi le vrai, je venais de plonger ici dans un de ces abîmes de solitude et de mutisme d'où l'on a peine à remonter, parce qu'on y égare, simplement, toute notion de temps." The suggestion that he accept a position at the Library of Congress to work with its collections of French literature has, however, aroused his interest: "C'est dans cet ordre d'idées que je puis envisager ici l'activité la plus conciliable avec ma situation particulière aussi bien qu'avec mes convenances personnelles et mes dispositions intimes."

193

Letter, 1940 Dec. 4, New York, N.Y., to [Archibald MacLeish, Washington, D.C.] [6] p. on 3 leaves. 24 cm.   Mss
    Holograph signed Alexis St. L. Leger.
    In the Archibald MacLeish papers.

Confirms his acceptance of an appointment at the Library and states his intention of settling in Washington early in January. Expressing his appreciation of the considerable administrative problems which MacLeish doubtless had to overcome in order to arrange matters for him, and his gratitude for the friendly spirit which has prompted these acts in his favor, he declares, "Je sais maintenant qu'il n'est plus besoin de mots entre nous, et que vous trouverez comme moi naturel de considerer notre amitié comme infiniment plus vieille que son acte de naissance." He is looking forward to the task awaiting him at the Library, where he hopes to preserve "le maximum de solitude, de silence et de repli sur moi." Concerned for the safety of his family in occupied France, he wishes to avoid any activities, such as lecturing, which would bring him to public notice.

194

Letter, 1941 Jan. 16, New York, N.Y., to [Archibald MacLeish, Washington, D.C.] [4] p. on 2 leaves. 24 cm.   CS
    Holograph signed Alexis St. L. Leger.
    In the Central Files.

Having delayed his departure from New York in order to meet a visitor bringing news from France, Leger is now unable to leave for Washington because all hotels have been completely booked for the inauguration. "Je n'aurais jamais pu imaginer que la Capitale fût exposée à de tels raz-de-marée. . . . Mes valises bouclées depuis Dimanche, j'attends le télégramme libérateur."

195

Memorandum, [1941 May 22? Washington, D.C., to Archibald Mac-Leish] the Librarian of Congress. 3 leaves. 27 cm.   Mss
    Holograph signed A. L.
    In the Archibald MacLeish papers.
    Comments on André Spire and his poetry.

196

Letter, 1941 June 9, [Washington, D.C., to Archibald MacLeish] [2] p. on 1 leaf. 27 cm.   CS
    Holograph signed Alexis Leger.
    In the Central Files.
A brief note concerning the visit of Alexander Schiffrin (a writer on political affairs and military strategy who used the pseudonym Max Werner).

197

Letter, 1941 Sept. 9, Washington, D.C., to Archibald MacLeish. [3] p. on 2 leaves. 27 cm.   PQ2623.E386E9   Rare Bk. Coll.
    Holograph signed A. L.
With the holograph of *Exil* (see item 29). Photocopy (negative) in the Archibald MacLeish papers (Mss).
Leger presents MacLeish with the fair copy of his poem *Exil*. Questioning whether it can be published in French in this country, he says, "Et elle serait intraduisible: non pas tant intellectuellement, dans ses abstractions, ses ellipses et ses ambiguités voulues, que physiquement, dans ses allitérations, ses assonances et ses incantations (astreintes au rhythme de la vague) — Littéralement aussi, dans les ressources étymologiques de certains de ses mots, les plus immatériels et les plus simples." An English translation of this extract was published in Arthur J. Knodel's *Saint-John Perse, a Study of His Poetry,* p. 97 (Edinburgh, At the University Press [1966] PQ2623.E386Z72), and in the *Quarterly Journal of the Library of Congress,* v. 27, Apr. 1970, p. 89 (Z881.U49A3, v. 27).

198

Letter, [1941] Sept. 19, [Washington, D.C.] to Archibald MacLeish.

[2] p. on 1 leaf.   27 cm.   Mss
   Holograph signed A. L.
   In the Archibald MacLeish papers.
Accompanies a letter from Lucien Vogel with a plan for the first issue of a new illustrated periodical, to be devoted to the arts of the Americas, on which MacLeish's views are sought.

199

Memorandum, 1941 Dec. 22, [Washington, D.C., to Archibald Mac-Leish] the Librarian of Congress. 2 leaves. 27 cm.   CS
   Typescript signed Alexis Leger.
   In the Central Files.
   Comments on English translations for an anthology of Spanish poetry.

200

Letter, 1941 Dec. 23, [Washington, D.C.] to Archibald MacLeish.
[6] p. on 3 leaves.   27 cm.   Mss
   Holograph signed Alexis St. L. Leger.
   In the Archibald MacLeish papers.
Discusses matters relating to the publication of his poetry in the United States and expresses the hope that MacLeish may eventually undertake the English translation of *Exil.* In supplying, at MacLeish's request, biographical and other personal information, some of which was translated into English and published in *Poetry,* v. 59, Mar. 1942 (see item 116), Leger comments, "Je ne puis malheureusement me faire à l'idée que le lecteur ait à rien connaître d'un auteur, tout au moins sur le plan absolu où l'œuvre poétique me semble devoir être libérée. Ce n'est pas par affectation ni calcul que j'ai toujours pratiqué si rigoureusement le dédoublement de personnalité." Nearly half this letter, with a number of minor changes, was published in *Cahiers de la pléiade,* no 10, été/automne 1950 (see item 115).

201

Memorandum, 1942 May 4, [Washington, D.C.] to Archibald Mac-Leish. 4 leaves. 27 cm.   CS
   Typescript (carbon copy) unsigned.
   In the Central Files.
   Gives particulars on the German translations of his poetry.

202

Letter, [1942] Aug. 15, [Washington, D.C.] to Archibald MacLeish.
[2] p. on 1 leaf.   28 cm.   CS
   Holograph signed Alexis L.
   In the Central Files.

Leger still hopes that MacLeish will translate *Exil*. He encloses the manuscript of a new poem *(Poème à l'étrangère)* and asks whether it could be typed, as he is thinking of sending it to some fellow country-men in New York who are founding a new poetry magazine and have asked him for a contribution to their first issue.

203

Letter, 1942 Aug. 19, [Washington, D.C.] to Archibald MacLeish.
1 p. 28 cm.   Mss
    Holograph signed A.
    In the Archibald MacLeish papers.

At MacLeish's answer to his letter of the 15th (described in the preceding entry), which indicated that he did not feel free to read the new poem without express permission, Leger responds, "C'est trop de raffinement dans la délicatesse (c'est tout vous!) Mon poème était bien d'abord pour vous. Que puis-je souhaiter d'autre que de vous avoir comme premier, ou même unique lecteur?" He continues, "Et ce poème, malgré mon horreur de tout poésie directe ou 'personnelle', est malgré moi, dans sa transposition, tout imprégné de ce Georgetown où je vis non loin de vous, où votre présence a pour moi tout son prix humain."

204

Letter, [1942 Aug. 26?] to Archibald MacLeish, [Washington, D.C.]
1 p. 28 cm.   CS
    Holograph signed A.
    In the Central Files.

Leger is on a train en route to a holiday with friends at 700 Acre Island, Dark Harbor, Maine. He feels he must remove himself from the Washington climate, if only for a short time, for the sake of his health. "J'essaierai de revenir digne de mon Boss, c'est à dire athlete complet sans talon d'Achille."

205

Letter, 1943 Feb. 24, [Washington, D.C.] to Archibald MacLeish. 3
leaves. 27 cm.   CS
    Holograph signed Alexis S. L. L.
    In the Central Files.

Excusing himself for not answering promptly, Leger says, "Mais tout papier à en-tête d'éditeur m'incite d'abord à l'évasion." Agrees to the request of W. W. Norton and Company for permission to publish a bi-lingual edition of *Eloges* and companion poems, using the English trans-lation made by Mme Edgar Varèse, and endorses Norton's suggestion that MacLeish contribute an introduction for American readers: "vous êtes le seul par qui je serais heureux et fier d'être 'présenté'."

206

Letter, 1943 Apr. 26, [Washington, D. C.] to Archibald MacLeish. 1 p. 27 cm.   CS

Holograph signed Alexis St. L. Leger.

In the Central Files.

Hopes that MacLeish's staff can handle the typing of the bibliography he has submitted (*A Selection of Works for an Understanding of World Affairs Since 1914*), should it be considered sufficiently useful to warrant the effort.

207

Letter, 1943 Aug. 21, [Washington, D.C.] to Archibald MacLeish. [2] p. on 1 leaf. 27 cm.   Mss

Holograph signed Alexis.

In the Archibald MacLeish papers.

Transmits an inscribed copy of *Exil* and announces his departure for a holiday at 700 Acre Island. Leger asks MacLeish to keep for him until his return the typescript of *Pluies* which is being prepared, as it will need numerous corrections.

208

Letter, 1944 Aug. 2, [Washington, D.C.] to Archibald MacLeish. [2] p. on 1 leaf. 28 cm.   Mss

Holograph signed A.

In the Archibald MacLeish papers.

Leger has been unwell and now intends to leave for his holiday at 700 Acre Island sooner than originally planned; he has been greatly upset by the receipt of bad news from France concerning close relatives and friends.

209

Letter, 1944 Oct. 6, [Washington, D.C.] to Archibald MacLeish. [4] p. on 2 leaves. 23 cm.   CS

Holograph signed A.

In the Central Files.

Transmits information just received about the investigation of Gallimard by a special commission examining the activities of all French publishers who continued to publish during the occupation.

210

Letter, 1944 Nov. 9, [Washington, D.C.] to Archibald MacLeish. [2] p. on 1 leaf. 28 cm.   Mss

Holograph signed A.

In the Archibald MacLeish papers.

Comments on the French translation, made by a Canadian, Roger Simond, of MacLeish's poem, "The Young Dead Soldiers."

211

Letter, 1944 Dec. 5, [Washington, D.C.] to Archibald MacLeish. [2] p. on 1 leaf. 28 cm.   Mss

Holograph signed A.

In the Archibald MacLeish papers.

Congratulates MacLeish (on his appointment as Assistant Secretary of State).

212

Memorandum, [1944 Dec. 20? Washington, D.C., to Archibald MacLeish] 1 p. 28 cm.   Mss

Holograph unsigned.

In the Archibald MacLeish papers.

Comments on a letter concerning contemporary French writers.

213

Letter, 1945 Apr. 23, [Washington, D.C.] to [Verner] Clapp, [Director of the Acquisitions Dept., Library of Congress] 1 p.   Z2161.L522

Photocopy (negative) of holograph signed Alexis St. L. Leger. In English. Original (not located) 27 or 28 cm. in height.

Bound with photocopy (negative) of incomplete first volume of his *La publication française pendant la guerre, bibliographie restreinte* (see item 189).

Transmits portions of the bibliography for use by the Library's purchasing agent in Paris.

214

Letter, 1946 Mar. 24, Washington, D.C., to Archibald MacLeish. [4] p. on 2 leaves. 28 cm.   Mss

Holograph signed Alexis.

In the Archibald MacLeish papers.

Leger wishes MacLeish well on the long holiday which he has embarked on, while mourning his removal from Washington. He would have liked MacLeish to read a new, long poem *(Vents)*, "auquel j'attache de l'importance, et où j'ai, dans une conception nouvelle, poussé plus loin que je ne l'ai jamais fait mes exigences envers moi-même." However, it had to be sent on to the Paris publisher. Should it be possible to get in touch with MacLeish before he rushes off once more, Leger will send him the proofs.

Memorandum, [1946 Nov. 1? Washington, D.C., to Luther Evans?]
[2] p. on 1 leaf. 28 cm.   CS
   Holograph unsigned.
   In the Central Files.
Draft of a statement for translation into English and signature by the
Librarian of Congress certifying Leger's unofficial status while serv-
ing as a consultant in French literature. A French translation of the
English version appears in *Honneur à Saint-John Perse,* p. 631 ([Paris]
Gallimard [1965] PQ2623.E386Z715).

216

Letter, 1947 July 1, Washington, D.C., to [Luther] Evans. [2] p. on
1 leaf. 28 cm.   CS
   Holograph signed Alexis Leger. In English.
   In the Central Files.
Requests advice and assistance in obtaining the refund of retirement
deductions.

217

Letter, 1947 Sept. 16, Washington, D.C., to [John C. L.] Andreassen,
[Director of the Administrative Department, Library of Congress] 1 p.
28 cm.   CS
   Holograph signed Alexis Leger. In English.
   In the Central Files.
Has just returned from a long holiday in Maine and is now submitting
the completed form required to handle his request for the refund of
retirement deductions.

218

Letter, [1947] Dec. 22, Washington, D.C., to Archibald MacLeish. 1 p.
27 cm.   Mss
   Holograph signed Alexis.
   In the Archibald MacLeish papers.
   Expresses condolence at the death of MacLeish's mother.

219

Letter, 1948 Nov. 12, Washington, D.C., to Archibald MacLeish. 4
leaves. 27 cm.   Mss
   Holograph signed Alexis.
   In the Archibald MacLeish papers.
Praises, at length and in some detail, MacLeish's latest book *(Act-five):*
"Vous avez su concilier là la pensée et le chant sans trahir les lois propres,
c'est à dire le mystère, de la création poétique." Conveys the news of

the death of his own mother, to whom, he says, "je devais tout ce que j'ai pu garder de foi dans la nature humaine."

220

Letter, 1949 June 18, Washington, D.C., to Archibald MacLeish. [4] p. on 2 leaves. 28 cm. **Mss**

Holograph signed Alexis.

In the Archibald MacLeish papers.

Leger expresses satisfaction at MacLeish's appointment (as Boylston Professor of Rhetoric and Oratory) at Harvard. A copy of a new book *(Exile, and Other Poems)*, just published by Pantheon, will be sent to MacLeish; it includes his introduction to *Eloges, and Other Poems,* of which Leger says, "Cette note est mon viatique dans votre pays, où la situation d'un écrivain étranger, aussi isolé que moi, est forcément ingrate. Votre témoignage ne chemine pas seulement en Amérique. En France même, et dans beaucoup d'autre pays d'Europe, je vois toujours citer quelque chose de vous dans les études qui me sont consacrées." However, "Tout cela vous expose à pire:" now MacLeish will be invited by Jean Paulhan to contribute to a special issue of *Cahiers de la pléiade* dedicated to Saint-John Perse. "On voudrait l'ouvrir aussi aux hommages étrangers—car en même temps, me dit-on, qu'on voudrait, pour la France, en faire l'occasion d'un 'groupement', ou regroupement littéraire, devenu necessaire, on voudrait y trouver lieu d'évoquer, autour de mon nom, certains problèmes de portée générale interessant aujourd'hui le langage aussi bien que la conception poétique." Discusses his plans to visit Cape Cod in July and spend August in Maine. Much effort is needed to complete a large-scale work, the most ambitious he has yet undertaken *(Amers).* "Je m'interdis en effet d'y céder tant que pèsent sur moi tristesse ou soucis, car je me suis juré, en défi à notre temps, de n'y accueillir que de la joie, libre et librement donnée."

221

Letter, 1949 July 23, Wellfleet, Cape Cod, Mass., to Archibald Mac-Leish. [3] p. on 2 leaves. 28 cm. **Mss**

Holograph signed Alexis.

In the Archibald MacLeish papers.

Leger is delighted at the generosity and appropriateness of MacLeish's contribution to the homage issue of *Cahiers de la pléiade.* "De vous, j'accepte une 'partialité' dont le jugement s'éclaire d'autant de cœur que d'esprit. Aussi bien ai-je appris depuis longtemps à n'aimer que la partialité, seul mode de connaissance que nous enseigne la Nature." He is pleased at the news that MacLeish is at work on a new poem. Leger would like to visit him at Conway and suggests the possibility of a stopover on his return to Washington from Maine. He adds, "Dites des choses amicales de ma part à Bullitt, à qui j'aurais de grand cœur lancé des œufs, non de poules ni même de dindes, mais de dinosaurs, pour lui apprendre à ne pas déserter l'amitié."

222

Letter, 1950 Apr. 10, Washington, D.C., to Archibald MacLeish. [2] p. on 1 leaf. 28 cm.   Mss
    Holograph signed A.
    In the Archibald MacLeish papers.
    Leger has evidently been informed that he is to receive the Award of Merit Medal for Poetry from the American Academy of Arts and Letters and wonders whether MacLeish has not had something to do with this: "Qu'avez-vous encore machiné-là, et conquis là, pour votre ami? Avec ce raffinement de discretion dont je connais bien la qualité?" He is moved by MacLeish's designation as his sponsor.

223

Letter, 1950 May 12, Washington, D.C., to Archibald MacLeish. [2] p. on 1 leaf. 28 cm.   Mss
    Holograph signed Alexis.
    In the Archibald MacLeish papers.
    Leger expresses gratitude for MacLeish's translation into English—a favor he had not dared to ask—of the acceptance speech which he intends to give in French at the American Academy's award ceremony.

224

Letter, [1950?] June 26, Washington, D.C., to Archibald MacLeish. [3] p. on 2 leaves. 28 cm.   Mss
    Holograph signed Alexis.
    In the Archibald MacLeish papers.
    As his summer plans include a visit to Ashfield, Mass., in August, following a cruise in Canadian waters, Leger hopes to see MacLeish at Conway.

225

Letter, 1952 Feb. 15, Washington, D.C., to Archibald MacLeish [Cambridge, Mass.?] [2] p. on 1 leaf. 28 cm.   Mss
    Holograph signed A.
    In the Archibald MacLeish papers.
    Leger has received a second invitation from the Charles Eliot Norton committee to lecture at Harvard and surmises that MacLeish prompted this: 'je mesure aujourd'hui tout le souci que vous avez dû garder du sort de votre difficile ami, jusqu'à cette nouvelle tentative en sa faveur.

Et je retrouve, là encore, l'aile fraternelle qui n'a cessé de veiller sur moi depuis douze ans." After considering the matter very carefully, Leger has decided again to refuse, as his contract with the Bollingen Foundation is to be renewed. Even though its stipend is much smaller, the Bollingen "m'assure du moins, pour l'immédiat, une liberté d'esprit dont j'ai encore besoin pour mon œuvre poétique en cours." He hopes that his decision will not put his friend into an awkward situation.

226

Letter, 1953 May 6, Washington, D.C., to [Archibald MacLeish] 1 p. 28 cm.   Mss

Holograph signed Alexis.

In the Archibald MacLeish papers.

Offers congratulations for several honors (one of them doubtless the Pulitzer Prize for poetry): "La main des hommes fait bien les choses, en ce moment, dans votre pays; et, ce faisant, elle j'honore d'abord elle-même."

227

Letter, 1953 June 30, Washington, D.C., to Archibald MacLeish. [2] p. on 1 leaf. 28 cm.   Mss

Holograph signed Alexis.

In the Archibald MacLeish papers.

"Dans la solitude qui semble croître autour de moi, et qui n'est pas seulement intellectuelle, quelle faveur des dieux m'aura valu ce beau rapport humain d'une amitié incomparable!" Hopes to see the MacLeishes while visiting at Ashfield during the summer. "J'ai, avec les Biddle, payé mon tribut à une insidieuse grippe d'été, du plus pur style Washingtonien, qui m'a laissé fatigué, mais le bon air de vos 'haut-lieux' me rendra vite mes jambes pour la marche."

228

Letter, [1954?] Feb. 18, Washington, D.C., to [Florence Cairns] [2] p. on 1 leaf. 28 cm.   Mss

Holograph signed Alexis L.

In the Huntington Cairns papers.

Sends thanks for a gift of flowers, which helped him to ward off gloom while he was bedridden. "J'aurais voulu vous remercier plus tôt, et de vive voix: une mauvaise grippe Washingtonienne m'a surpris, déjà fatigué, dès mon retour chez moi, et pour ne pas accabler encore l'affectueuse sollicitude de bons amis comme vous, je n'ai su, écœuré de moi-même, que me condamner au silence et à la solitude. Je pars demain pour le Sud et vais demander au voisinage de la mer la possibilité de me libérer, par la natation, des dernières traces de mon accident."

229

Letter, [1954] Nov. 8, Washington, D.C., to George Biddle. 2 leaves. 28 cm. Mss
Holograph signed Alexis.
In the George Biddle and Hélène Sardeau papers.
An expression of condolence on the death of Biddle's brother Sydney.

230

Letter, 1954 Nov. 28, Washington, D.C., to Hélène Biddle. 2 leaves. 28 cm. Mss
Holograph signed Alexis.
In the George Biddle and Hélène Sardeau papers.
"Le beau dessin que je tiens de vos mains s'imprégne beaucoup de votre propre sensibilité, et l'art qui s'y exprime vous est propre. Il y a là, avec aisance et fatalisme, une belle certitude. Merci de la délicatesse avec laquelle vous me l'offrez."

231

Letter, [1958] Apr. 25, Washington, D.C., to Archibald MacLeish. 3 leaves. 28 cm. Mss
Holograph signed Alexis.
In the Archibald MacLeish papers.
Never has Leger so much regretted the distance separating him from the MacLeishes—he is to be married next day (to Dorothy Milburn Russell) and wishes that MacLeish could attend as a witness with Francis (Biddle). "Ami très cher, l'Amérique m'avait déjà beaucoup donné en me donnant 'mon frère Archie': elle achève de me combler en me donnant aujourd'hui une compagne digne de l'affection de ceux qui me sont vraiment proches." Leger has acquired a house in France, on the Mediterranean coast, and plans an extended stay there with his wife. "Mais je ne l'enlève pas à l'Amérique, car j'y reviendrai tous les ans avec elle pour sept mois, et j'y garde ma résidence officielle."

232

Letter, 1958 May 14, Washington, D.C., to Huntington Cairns. 3 leaves. 28 cm. Mss
Holograph signed Alexis. In English.
In the Huntington Cairns papers.
At Cairns' suggestion, Leger encloses some notices of *Amers* clipped from French periodicals for the use of any American critic whom Cairns might interest in preparing a serious review of the English translation,

Seamarks, scheduled to appear in early July, "which is not a favorable literary season." Leger comments on the paucity of reviews of his last work, *Winds,* which was not mentioned even in the journals that had been authorized to print lengthy extracts of the poem in advance of its publication in book form.

233
Letter, [1958] May 14, Washington, D.C., to Archibald MacLeish. 4 leaves. 28 cm. Mss
Holograph signed A.
In the Archibald MacLeish papers.
Leger has postponed his visit to France pending clarification of the political situation there. He expresses his pleasure at the success of MacLeish's play *(J. B.)* and comments, "Il me semble que cela prend l'allure d'un véritable événement littéraire. Vous relevez enfin, en notre temps, cette notion d'"œuvre', que l'on a trop tendance à déserter parmi l'émiettement littéraire. Et il me semble que votre maîtrise de langue a surmonté là, très remarquablement, les plus sérieuses difficultés en fait de mouvement, d'activité et de densité dans la métrique du langage poétique au théâtre contemporain." As in the letter to Huntington Cairns of the same date (described in the preceding entry), he encloses clippings of French reviews of *Amers,* in the hope that MacLeish may find someone in his literary or scholarly circles who would be willing to review the English translation. He insists, however, that MacLeish is not to undertake the task himself; his contributions have already been so frequent and so generous that Leger does not wish to distract him for a single moment from his own writing.

234
Letter, 1959 Apr. 7, Washington, D.C., to Huntington Cairns. 1 p. 28 cm. Mss
Holograph signed A. L. In English.
In the Huntington Cairns papers.
A short note accompanying the carbon copy of a letter (described in the following entry) to the director of the Bollingen Foundation, concerning the settlement of an income tax refund claim.

235
Letter, 1959 Apr. 7, [Washington, D.C.] to John D. Barrett, New York, N.Y. 2 leaves. 28 cm. Mss
Typescript (carbon copy) unsigned. In English.
In the Huntington Cairns papers.

77

Discusses problems arising from the payment by the Internal Revenue Service of a claim for refund of income tax paid eight years earlier.

236

Letter, 1959 May 5, New York, N.Y., to Archibald MacLeish. 1 p. 28 cm. Mss

Holograph signed Alexis.

In the Archibald MacLeish papers.

Congratulates MacLeish on a new honor (perhaps the Antoinette Perry Award in Drama for *J. B.*). "Et il est bien d'avoir donné, contre tous risques, l'exemple d'une 'œuvre' véritable et de haute visée, à l'heure où l'impuissance littéraire cherche son refuge dans une fragmentation de plus en plus vaine de l'immédiat et du fortuit."

237

Letter, 1960 Feb. 8, Washington, D.C., to Archibald MacLeish. 3 leaves. 28 cm. Mss

Holograph signed A.

In the Archibald MacLeish papers.

Asks MacLeish's advice concerning the English translation of *Chronique* and expresses satisfaction at the news, received from a mutual friend, of MacLeish's improving health. In a postscript, he adds, "La mort du pauvre Camus a été un gros choc pour tout mon milieu d'amis littéraires à Paris. J'étais en train de clore une lettre pour lui quand l'affreuse nouvelle m'a atteint par la radio."

238

Letter, 1960 Feb. 26, Washington, D.C., to Archibald MacLeish. 2 leaves. 28 cm. Mss

Holograph signed A.

In the Archibald MacLeish papers.

Leger has been surprised by the news of his election as an honorary member of the American Academy of Arts and Letters and the National Institute of Arts and Letters, and attributes this fresh distinction to the initiative of his friend. Although he was informed that the insignia and the citation could be sent to him if this would be more convenient, he feels it would be "inélégant" not to attend the induction ceremony. He is leaving shortly for a visit to Argentina, upon the official invitation of the Argentine Government; he plans to return via Chile and Peru and to embark for France not earlier than mid-June.

239

Letter, 1960 May 16, New York, N.Y., to Archibald MacLeish. [2] p. on 1 leaf. 27 cm. Mss

Holograph signed A.

In the Archibald MacLeish papers.

Leger has arrived in New York to participate in the ceremonies of the American Academy on May 25. He expects to return to Washington a few days afterward to prepare for the journey to France, and hopes that before his departure he will hear good news about MacLeish's health. He gives a brief résumé of his Argentine visit.

240

Letter, [1960] May 31, New York, N.Y., to Archibald MacLeish. 1 p. 28 cm. Mss

Holograph signed A.

In the Archibald MacLeish papers.

In a brief note written before catching his train to Washington, Leger reports that he has now received favorable news about the renewal of his Bollingen fellowship and is greatly moved by MacLeish's efforts to inquire into the matter on his behalf. He praises MacLeish's article on the American moral crisis, just published in *Life*.

241

Cablegram, 1960 Oct. 28, Hyères, Var, to Archibald MacLeish, Cambridge, Mass. 1 p. 15 x 21 cm. Mss

In the Archibald MacLeish papers.

Message reads: "Pour vous, mon frère Archie, toute mon affectueuse et réconnaissante pensée, Alexis." Probably a response to a congratulatory message upon the announcement of the Nobel award.

242

Letter, [1961] Feb. 28, Washington, D.C., to Huntington Cairns. [2] p. on 1 leaf. 28 cm. Mss

Holograph signed Alexis L.

In the Huntington Cairns papers.

Expresses his pleasure at their meeting the previous day and encloses a critical study of *Poésie* ("Critique de la critique," by Manuel de Diéguez, published in *Combat*, 19. année, 19 jan. 1961, p. 6) which he had talked of when they met. He had at first thought of suggesting that it be included in the Bollingen series edition of *Poésie* but, on further consideration, he has decided against such a step.

Two photocopies of the *Combat* article are attached.

243

Letter, 1967 Feb. 21, Washington, D.C., to Archibald MacLeish. [4] p. on 2 leaves. 28 cm. Mss

Holograph signed Alexis.

In the Archibald MacLeish papers.

Begins with an expression of sadness at losing touch with an old friend ("L'âge s'accroît, l'ombre s'allonge sous nos pas . . . "). Suggests the possibility that they may meet, either in the Caribbean, where Leger plans to visit friends on Barbuda for a week in March, or in New York, where he will spend the first fortnight in April. "Quoi qu'il en soit, ma pensée s'envolera souvent vers vous, de Barbuda, et je saurai me faire 'Zombi' ou Frigate Bird pour survoler en songe Antigua, comme je le fais chaque fois qu'un retour en mer Caraïbe me rapproche de votre île. J'y laisserai tomber pour vous mon affectueux message, inscrit sur feuille de 'sea-grape' comme au temps de vos 'Conquistadors'." Leger states that Gallimard is planning a critical edition of his work in the Pléiade series and has requested a selection of letters written during the years he spent in America. He asks MacLeish whether he has retained any of those sent him, and if copies could be made. "J'aimerais beaucoup que votre nom peut figurer, dans ce livre auquel je cède tardivement, parmi ceux qui ont le plus signifié et continuent de signifier le plus pour moi, intellectuellement et humainement."

OTHER PUBLISHED LECTURES PRESENTED UNDER THE AUSPICES OF THE GERTRUDE CLARKE WHITTALL POETRY AND LITERATURE FUND

These brochures, published by the Library of Congress, may be purchased from the Superintendent of Documents, Government Printing Office, Washington, D.C. 20402, for 25 cents each, with the exceptions noted below.

AMERICAN POETRY AT MID-CENTURY. 1958. 49 p. *Out of print.*
New Poets and Old Muses, by John Crowe Ransom. The Present State of Poetry, by Delmore Schwartz. The Two Knowledges, by John Hall Wheelock.

ANNI MIRABILES, 1921–1925: Reason in the Madness of Letters, by Richard P. Blackmur. 1956. 55 p. *Out of print.*

ANNIVERSARY LECTURES. 1959. 56 p.
Robert Burns, by Robert S. Hillyer. The House of Poe, by Richard Wilbur. Alfred Edward Housman, by Cleanth Brooks.

THE ART OF HISTORY. Two Lectures. 1967. 38 p.
The Old History and the New, by Allan Nevins. Biography, History, and the Writing of Books, by Catherine Drinker Bowen.

CARL SANDBURG. By Mark Van Doren. With a Bibliography of Sandburg Materials in the Collections of the Library of Congress. 1969. 83 p. *50 cents.*

DANTE ALIGHIERI. Three Lectures. 1965. 53 p.
The Interest in Dante Shown by Nineteenth-Century American Men of Letters, by J. Chesley Mathews. On Reading Dante in 1965: the *Divine Comedy* as a "Bridge Across Time," by Francis Fergusson. The Relevance of the *Inferno,* by John Ciardi.

FRENCH AND GERMAN LETTERS TODAY. Four Lectures. 1960. 53 p. *Out of print.*
Lines of Force in French Poetry, by Pierre Emmanuel. Latest Trends in French Prose, by Alain Bosquet. The Modern German Mind: the Legacy of Nietzsche, by Erich Heller. Crossing the Zero Point: German Literature Since World War II, by Hans Egon Holthusen.

GEORGE BERNARD SHAW, Man of the Century, by Archibald Henderson. 1957. 15 p. *Out of print.*

THE IMAGINATION IN THE MODERN WORLD. Three Lectures, by Stephen Spender. 1962. 40 p. *Out of print.*
The Imagination as Verb. The Organic, the Orchidaceous, the Intellectualized. Imagination Means Individuation.

PERSPECTIVES: Recent Literature of Russia, China, Italy, and Spain. Four Lectures. 1961. 57 p. *Out of print.*
Russian Soviet Literature Today, by Marc Slonim. Chinese Letters Since the Literary Revolution (1917), by Lin Yutang. The Progress of Realism in the Italian Novel, by Giose Rimanelli. The Contemporary Literature of Spain, by Arturo Torres-Rioseco.

RANDALL JARRELL, by Karl Shapiro. With a bibliography of Jarrell Materials in the Collections of the Library of Congress. 1967. 47 p.

RECENT AMERICAN FICTION, by Saul Bellow. 1963. 12 p. *15 cents.*

ROBERT FROST: A Backward Look, by Louis Untermeyer. With a Selective Bibliography. 1964. 40 p.

THREE VIEWS OF THE NOVEL. 1957. 41 p. *Out of print.*
The Biographical Novel, by Irving Stone. Remarks on the Novel, by John O'Hara. The Historical Novel, by MacKinlay Kantor.

WALT WHITMAN: Man, Poet, Philosopher. 1955, reissued 1969. 53 p.
The Man, by Gay Wilson Allen. The Poet, by Mark Van Doren. The Philosopher, by David Daiches.

WILLA CATHER: The Paradox of Success, by Leon Edel. 1960. 17 p. *Out of print.*

THE WRITER'S EXPERIENCE. 1964. 32 p. 20 cents. *Out of print.*
Hidden Names and Complex Fate: A Writer's Experience in the United States, by Ralph Ellison. American Poet? by Karl Shapiro.

☆ U.S. GOVERNMENT PRINTING OFFICE: 1971 O—422—495